"In a world that is often confused about prayer, any book that helps Catholics to pray is a boon to the Church. Scott Hahn, in the first part of this book, draws on the experience of his own journey of faith, which led him to the Catholic Church, and on the wisdom of the Church Fathers to throw light on the essential spirit of prayer found in the Our Father. He also gently sets aside false approaches. The extracts from Saints Cyprian, Cyril of Jerusalem, John Chrysostom, and Augustine, which make up the second part of the book, are a precious source of insight into Christian prayer. I hope the book will be used by many families, for those who use it will find their life with God strengthened and enriched."

+FRANCIS CARDINAL GEORGE, O.M.I., D.D., PH.D., S.T.D.
Former Archbishop of Chicago

"My own journey into the Catholic Church involved an exponential increase in praying the Lord's Prayer, from once a week on Sundays to multiple times every day: the Divine Office, rosaries, and Mass. But I must admit that too often the busyness and distractions of my life have made my recitation of this precious prayer exactly what Jesus warned against: 'vain repetitions.' In this sense, therefore, Scott's book was a godsend. His theological, biblical, and spiritually informed reflections (petition by petition) on this intimate family prayer of the Body of Christ have instilled new life into this dead old soul. What an awesome privilege it is to pray these words as an adopted son of God, taught by our adopted Brother, Jesus, Who is also our Lord and God, Savior and King."

MARCUS GRODI
President, Coming Home Network International

"Against the background of contemporary misunderstandings of God and Christian revelation, it is gratifying to see how a modern Scripture scholar, Professor Scott Hahn, contributes concise and profound insights into the most familiar prayer in all history, the Lord's Prayer. His meditations, enriched by covenant theology, will inspire souls with greater knowledge and love of God, Who is the Blessed Trinity, and will stimulate in them a greater zeal to spread Christ's Kingdom, the Church, on earth. Readers victimized by a spiritually decadent culture to ignore their supernatural destiny are reminded, 'If He Who was without sin prayed, how much more ought sinners to pray.' The value of this volume is enhanced by inclusion of the texts of timeless commentaries on the Lord's Prayer by Saints Cyprian, Cyril of Jerusalem, John Chrysostom, and Augustine."

JAMES LIKOUDIS
President Emeritus, Catholics United for the Faith

"This is a great book for all Catholics, but it is an essential book for Catholic fathers. At the center of the modern crisis in family life is a crisis of genuine fatherhood. The essence of restoring fatherhood is turning the hearts of fathers back to God the Father. The renewal of family life will proceed from the renewal of our life with the Father. Read this important book slowly and prayerfully. It will deepen your faith and transform your family life."

STEVE WOOD
Founder, St. Joseph's Covenant Keepers

Praise for *Understanding "Our Father"*

"In *Understanding 'Our Father,'* Dr. Scott Hahn removes the veil and reveals to us the deep significance of the prayer Jesus gave us, the Our Father. With elegance, eloquence, and erudite scholarship, Dr. Hahn unpacks each phrase of this perfect prayer and shows us our relationship with God the Father, His providential care for us, and our own call to be divinized by following His holy will. This book has increased my understanding and enriched my appreciation of the Our Father, and I am sure this will be the case for everyone who reads this insightful and inspiring book."

JOHNETTE S. BENKOVIC
President and Founder, Women of Grace

"In this wonderful exposition of the most beautiful of human prayers, that prayer which came from the divine lips of Jesus Christ Himself, Dr. Scott Hahn has, once again, provided the Catholic and the Christian with a splendid work of theological research. *Understanding 'Our Father'* will definitely serve to enrich spiritually all who are privileged to read and meditate on it. By coordinating his commentary and meditation on the Lord's Prayer with those of four great doctors of the Church, Dr. Hahn provides an ongoing connection with the long continuity of Christian tradition. It is a book that the reader will find as intellectually satisfying as it is grace-filled and consoling."

MOST REV. FABIAN W. BRUSKEWITZ, D.D., S.T.D.
Bishop Emeritus of Lincoln

"Scott Hahn brings excitement and scholarship to his inspirational work on the Lord's Prayer. Once again, Scott takes what is familiar to us and, with refreshing insight, inspires us to renewed zeal."

REV. MICHAEL SCANLAN, T.O.R.
Former Chancellor, Franciscan University of Steubenville

UNDERSTANDING
"OUR FATHER"

UNDERSTANDING "OUR FATHER"

Biblical Reflections on the Lord's Prayer

EMMAUS
ROAD
PUBLISHING

Steubenville, Ohio
www.EmmausRoad.org

SCOTT HAHN

Emmaus Road Publishing
1468 Parkview Circle
Steubenville, Ohio 43952

Library of Congress Control Number: 2002111427
ISBN 1-931018-15-4
ISBN 978-1-931018-15-9

Cover design by Emily Feldkamp | Layout by Beth Hart

Cover artwork:
Pompeo Batoni, *God the Father*

Nihil obstat: Rev. James Dunfee, *Censor Librorum*
Imprimatur: Ñ R. Daniel Conlon, D.D., J.C.D., Ph.D.
Bishop of Steubenville
August 29, 2002

The *nihil obstat* and *imprimatur* are official declarations
that a book or pamphlet is free of doctrinal or moral error.
No implication is contained therein that those who have
granted the *nihil obstat* and *imprimatur* agree with
the contents, opinions, or statements expressed.

"Wisdom from the Fathers of the Church" is a modernized adaptation of selec-
tions of four works in the public domain: Saint Cyprian, *Treatise IV (On the
Lord's Prayer)*, in *Ante-Nicene Fathers*, vol. 5, ed. Alexander Roberts and James
Donaldson (1886); Saint Cyril of Jerusalem, *Lecture XXIII*, in *Nicene and
Post-Nicene Fathers*, 2d ser., vol. 7, ed. Philip Schaff and Henry Wace (1894);
Saint John Chrysostom, *Homily XIX on the Gospel of St. Matthew*, in *Nicene
and Post-Nicene Fathers*, 1st ser., vol. 10, ed. Philip Schaff (1888); and Saint
Augustine, *Our Lord's Sermon on the Mount*, in *Nicene and Post-Nicene Fathers*,
1st ser., vol. 6, ed. Philip Schaff (1888). These works are available online at
http://www.ccel.org.

To Don Javier Echevarria,
bishop, prelate, priest . . .
and my father.

CONTENTS

— PART II —
WISDOM FROM THE FATHERS OF THE CHURCH

ACKNOWLEDGMENTS

I feel obligated here to thank several people whom God has sent in answer to my prayers. Without them, I could not have completed this volume; nor could you be holding it now. Thank you, Jeff Ziegler, for editing the translations of the patristic texts; Mike Aquilina, for editing my manuscript; and Beth Hart, for designing a beautiful book.

ABBREVIATIONS

The Old Testament

Gen./Genesis
Ex./Exodus
Lev./Leviticus
Num./Numbers
Deut./Deuteronomy
Josh./Joshua
Judg./Judges
Ruth/Ruth
1 Sam./1 Samuel
2 Sam./2 Samuel
1 Kings/1 Kings
2 Kings/2 Kings
1 Chron./1 Chronicles
2 Chron./2 Chronicles
Ezra/Ezra
Neh./Nehemiah
Tob./Tobit
Jud./Judith
Esther/Esther
Job/Job
Ps./Psalms
Prov./Proverbs
Eccles./Ecclesiastes
Song/Song of Solomon
Wis./Wisdom
Sir./Sirach (Ecclesiasticus)
Is./Isaiah
Jer./Jeremiah
Lam./Lamentations
Bar./Baruch

Ezek./Ezekiel
Dan./Daniel
Hos./Hosea
Joel/Joel
Amos/Amos
Obad./Obadiah
Jon./Jonah
Mic./Micah
Nahum/Nahum
Hab./Habakkuk
Zeph./Zephaniah
Hag./Haggai
Zech./Zechariah
Mal./Malachi
1 Mac./1 Maccabees
2 Mac./2 Maccabees

The New Testament

Mt./Matthew
Mk./Mark
Lk./Luke
Jn./John
Acts/Acts of the Apostles
Rom./Romans
1 Cor./1 Corinthians
2 Cor./2 Corinthians
Gal./Galatians
Eph./Ephesians
Phil./Philippians
Col./Colossians
1 Thess./1 Thessalonians

2 Thess./2 Thessalonians
1 Tim./1 Timothy
2 Tim./2 Timothy
Tit./Titus
Philem./Philemon
Heb./Hebrews
Jas./James
1 Pet./1 Peter
2 Pet./2 Peter
1 Jn./1 John
2 Jn./2 John
3 Jn./3 John
Jude/Jude
Rev./Revelation (Apocalypse)

— PART I —

CONTEMPORARY REFLECTIONS BY SCOTT HAHN

A GOSPEL PRAYER

The prayer at hand has been called many things: the *Pater Noster*, the Our Father, the Model Prayer, the Lord's Prayer. Some people object to calling it the Lord's Prayer because Jesus committed no trespasses, and so He could not ask forgiveness, He could not pray this prayer as His own. They call it the Disciple's Prayer.

Whatever you choose to call it, one thing is certain: It's a prayer of paramount importance. It is the centerpiece of "the most famous sermon ever preached"—the Sermon on the Mount. Not only is this the most famous sermon, it's also the first we find Jesus preaching when we read the Gospel. It's three chapters long (Mt. 5-7)—no typical homily here! And those three chapters contain one thing we won't find anywhere in the first four chapters of Matthew: that is, God's fatherhood. From no references at all, Jesus proceeds, in the course of His sermon, to make seventeen references to God as Father. He evokes many other family images as well: marriage, wife, brother, children, house-building, and so on.

It should come as no surprise, then, that the opening words of the centerpiece prayer of the most famous sermon in history are "Our Father."

Fatherhood is just the beginning; family is the context. All of that is quite familiar to us. Indeed, we may have heard it too much—or, more precisely, we may have pondered it too little. If so, then we have to change.

Often we're tempted to consider the Lord's Prayer as a kind of inspired but ad hoc arrangement, improvised by our Lord on the spot as a quick reply to an unexpected request. We grant that it's very good, of course—since it came from Jesus Himself—but we don't trouble ourselves to find a structure or an inner logic in something so spontaneous.

That approach, however, is completely mistaken. The Lord's Prayer reflects Jesus' deepest preoccupation on earth: talking with His Father. It moves smoothly from there to His second deepest preoccupation: making His Father our Father too, enabling us to share His intimate conversation, which is constant and habitual. Without a doubt, the Lord's Prayer is more than a sudden inspiration on Jesus' part. It's a long-awaited gift. Indeed, this prayer is itself an answer to a sustained request on the part of humanity: "Lord, teach us to pray" (Lk 11:1).

Indeed, the very desire to pray, and the request for instruction, were assuredly answers to Jesus' own prayers. If Jesus prayed all night before choosing the twelve followers who would be His inner circle of disciples, then He must have been praying for days and weeks that these men would become *true* disciples. That couldn't happen without a lot of prayer, and not just Jesus' prayers, but theirs, too. The disciples needed prayer more than they needed a walking staff, or sandals, or clothing, or a wallet, or fish, or food, or drink. So they had to learn to pray like Jesus, in the very words that Jesus would have them pray, in the very way that Jesus Himself prayed.

And that brings us back to the Our Father.

The Lord's Prayer is one unified, compact, model prayer consisting of seven petitions, divisible into two parts: the first "God-ward," the second "us-ward." No work of poetic art was ever more perfectly crafted. If we had more time, we could consider how the prayer's sevenfold pattern is reflected in the seven parables of Matthew 13, in the seven woes of Matthew 23, and in the Beatitudes.[1] But such a discussion would turn this book into a scholarly monograph and not a meditation.

Still, if you want to see how the Our Father changes the souls who use it in prayer, take a closer look at its structure. The first part is clearly "God-ward," focused on "Thy name," "Thy Kingdom," "Thy will." The second half, however, turns attention to us and our needs: "give us," "forgive us," "lead us," "deliver us." The sequence is significant, because it reverses the instinctive order of our petitions. When we pray spontaneously, we tend to begin with our troubles, our frustrated desires, and our personal wish list. But Jesus shows us that we need to be less self-centered in prayer and more God-centered—not because God needs our praise, and His ego is fragile, but because He's God, and we aren't. In its very sequence, the Our Father is a much-needed orientation-to-reality program.

I hope this book is an answer to your prayers and our Lord's prayer for you. For He still wants the same things for His disciples: He wants to make His Father our Father.

OUR FATHER

I was a college student, still a teenager, and still savoring my recent experience of conversion. I had been "born again," saved by Christ from sins that would have destroyed me, and I was eager to share my faith with other kids who seemed headed for delinquency.

So I jumped at the chance for a summer internship in the inner city, helping to run youth programs for adolescents who lived in poverty. The ministry was run by two tough young men who had themselves converted after spending years in street gangs. One had been a member of the militant Black Panthers.

Their misspent youth was a providential preparation for ministry in that part of town—where most storefronts were boarded up, and drug dealers and police cruisers were the most frequent visitors. They talked tough to me on my first day and showed me to the spartan room where I'd be spending my nights. On one particular night, fairly early in the summer, I was on my knees praying in that room, when I heard gunfire outside and bullets whizzing by my window. Still, I have to say that I was happy to be there. The squalor and the danger made me all the more aware of the neighborhood's need for Jesus Christ.

Father-Hunger

Weeks passed before the directors of the ministry felt confident enough to let me give inspirational talks to the boys. They prepped me once more by making sure I was truly aware of the boys' home lives. Most, they said, came from single-parent households. Many didn't even know the names of their fathers. Some had fathers who were in prison—or dead, the victims of their own criminal lifestyle.

My directors had spent their entire lives in neighborhoods like this. They evoked a bleak picture of a subculture that had no experience or recent memory of fathers being involved in family life. And they brought all this to a practical point: "When you talk to these kids, don't talk about God as their Father. That's something they can't relate to. It can only turn them off."

I was stunned. How could a Christian talk about God without mentioning His fatherhood?

I had finally arrived at the moment I was dreaming of—the day when I could preach the Gospel to kids who were "at risk"—and I knew that I couldn't do it the way my directors wanted me to do it.

So I asked them, How could I lead our group to the Son of God without mentioning His eternal Father? And how could I lead them to pray except in the way that Jesus had taught us: "Our Father"?

I made an impassioned case, and I guess I convinced them, because they agreed to let me try it my way.

I did, and my directors had to acknowledge that I succeeded. When I spoke of God as Father, I spoke not to the memories of my audience, but to their need. They hungered for a father more than they hungered for a good meal. They knew what they'd been missing, and they were eager to find it in God.

There is only one God. He is the God Whom Jesus revealed to us, and He is the God Who made the hearts of those adolescent boys. God made us for Himself, said Saint Augustine, and our hearts are restless till they rest in Him—the only true God.[1]

Father Forever

As a young Evangelical Protestant, I had read the words of the Anglican theologian J. I. Packer: "For everything that Christ taught . . . is summed up in the knowledge of the Fatherhood of God. 'Father' is the Christian name for God."[2]

As a superannuating Catholic, I turn to the words of Tertullian. This third-century African Christian wrote that before Jesus Christ "[t]he expression God the Father had never been revealed to anyone. When Moses himself asked God who he was, he heard another name. The Father's name has been revealed to us in the Son, for the name 'Son' implies the new name 'Father.'"[3]

Since the name lay hidden till Jesus, it was new to mankind with the New Testament. But it was not newly coined. For God's name, from all eternity, is Father.

Jesus revealed this at the end of His earthly ministry, when He commanded His disciples to baptize "in

---

[1] Cf. Saint Augustine, *Confessions*, bk. 1, chap. 1, no. 1.
[2] J. I. Packer, *Evangelical Magazine* 7: 19 ff., quoted in J. I. Packer, *Knowing God* (Downers Grove, Ill.: InterVarsity Press, 1973), 182.
[3] Tertullian, *De Oratione* (On Prayer), chap. 3, quoted in Catechism, no. 2779.

the name of the Father and of the Son and of the Holy Spirit" (Mt. 28:19).

What Jesus named here was radically different from anything the world has seen, before or since. Other religions have invoked their gods as father, but they have used the title only in a metaphorical sense—meaning that their god is *like* a father, because he begets them, guides them, and provides for them.

Jesus praised God as Begetter, Guide, and Provider, but He also—by His own eternal sonship—named God as eternally Father. For *Father* can be God's name, His personal identity, only if God is Father eternally.

Think about the other titles we give God—Creator, Lawgiver, and Physician. He is Creator only *after* He has created something; so Creator is not God's personal identity. He is Lawgiver only *after* He has given a law; so He is not an eternal lawgiver. He is Physician only *after* He has creatures in need of healing.

Yet He is Father forever, because He eternally generates the Son, and together They breathe forth the Spirit, the bond of Their love.[4]

A Family Affair

The eternal relation of the Father and the Son is not a metaphor. Indeed, human fatherhood is more like a metaphor for God's eternal fatherhood. Human fatherhood is a created image of God's eternal fatherhood—an image more or less vivid, depending on the sins of the dad.

---

[4] See my *First Comes Love: Finding Your Family in the Church and the Trinity* (New York: Doubleday, 2002), chap. 3-5.

Saint Ephrem of Syria put it well. Earthly fathers, he said, "are called fathers, but He is the true Father. . . . The terms 'father' and 'son' by which they have been called are borrowed names that through grace have taught us that there is a single true Father and that He has a single true Son."[5]

God is Father to Jesus, Who shares His sonship with us. In the Church's ancient phrase, we are made "sons in the Son" through baptism. We become, quite literally, partakers of the divine nature (cf. 2 Pet. 1:4). We are made godlike. We are made to share in the love Christ shares with the Father. Only when we grasp this can we truly pray, "I shall not want" (Ps. 23:1). We'll want for nothing because the Lord is not just our Shepherd, but also our Father. And someone who lives the life of God ultimately needs nothing other than that life.

God is our Father because we share in Jesus' sonship. Note that we do not address Him as "my Father," but as "our Father." By gathering us together in Christ, God has established a universal human family in the Church. In the words of Pope John Paul II, "The Father, Creator of the universe, and the Word Incarnate, the Redeemer of humanity, are the source of this universal openness to all people as brothers and sisters, and they impel us to *embrace them in the prayer* which begins with the tender words: *'Our Father.'*"[6] It is our common sonship that gives us the right to address God as a common Father, as *our* Father.

---

[5] Saint Ephrem, *Hymn 46 on the Faith*, quoted in Andrew Louth, *Denys the Areopagite* (Wilton, Conn.: Morehouse-Barlow, 1989), 80.

[6] Pope John Paul II, Letter to Families *Gratissimam Sane* (February 2, 1994), no. 4, emphasis in original.

All the remaining words in the Lord's Prayer—indeed, all the truths of the Christian faith—can be understood as an elaboration of that compact opening phrase: "Our Father."

CHAPTER TWO

OUR FATHER…IN HEAVEN

If we want to be Christians, we have no choice but to pray, "Our Father." When the first disciples asked Jesus to teach them to pray, He taught them using those very words. To pray as a Christian means to pray, "Our Father."

Yet, as I learned in my first days of ministry, the word *father* has become a stumbling block for some people. Divorce is common, as is birth outside wedlock. I live in a country that one popular book described as fatherless America.[1] So, for a growing number of people, father has never meant provider, teacher, or guardian. It has meant only an aching absence—or an abusive presence.

Moreover, even children who have grown up with a good father are all too aware of his defects, problems, and sins. The best intentions of the most virtuous dads too often get botched in execution. What we human fathers wouldn't give our kids! But we don't always have what they want or need; and, when we do have it, we don't know how to give it to them without spoiling them.

---

[1] David Blankenhorn, *Fatherless America: Confronting Our Most Urgent Social Problem* (New York: Harper Collins, 1996).

The "Our" of Power

This is why Tradition tells us we must go beyond our earthly experiences and memories of fatherhood when we pray, "Our Father." For though He is a provider, begetter, and protector, God is more *unlike* than *like* any human father, patriarch, or paternal figure. The Catechism puts it this way: "God our Father transcends the categories of the created world. To impose our own ideas in this area 'upon him' would be to fabricate idols to adore or pull down. To pray to the Father is to enter into his mystery as he is and as the Son has revealed him to us" (no. 2779).

How has Jesus, God the Son, revealed the Father to us? As "[o]ur Father who art in heaven" (Mt. 6:9). By adding that prepositional phrase "in heaven," Jesus emphasizes the difference in God's fatherhood. The Father to Whom we pray is not an earthly father. He is "above" us; He is the One we profess in the creed as "Father Almighty"—that is, all powerful. Though we are weak, limited, and prone to mistakes, nothing is impossible for God (cf. Lk. 1:37).

God's power, then, sets His fatherhood apart from any fatherhood we have known or imagined. His "fatherhood and power shed light on one another" (Catechism, no. 270). Unlike earthly fathers, He always has the best intentions for His children, and He always has the ability to carry them out. Jesus wanted us to know this, so that we could always approach our heavenly Father with childlike trust and confidence: "[W]hatever you ask in prayer, you will receive, if you have faith" (Mt. 21:22).

The Catechism teaches that "God reveals his fatherly omnipotence by the way he takes care of our needs" (no. 270). We know God as Father because, over a lifetime of prayer, we experience His care for us. We come to see for ourselves that He is mighty, and that He will deny us nothing that is good for us.

From Heir to Paternity

Earthly fatherhood sometimes reflects these characteristics, as do those offices that assume fatherly roles in society: the priesthood, for example, and the government. Yet earthly fathers can perfect their fatherhood only by purifying themselves of earthly motives—such as greed, envy, pride, and the desire to control. They can become true fathers only by conforming themselves to the image of their heavenly Father, and that Image is His firstborn Son, Jesus Christ.

In governing, in parenting, or in priesthood, we come to exercise a more perfect fatherly role as we "grow up" in the Family of God: "[W]e are children of God, and if children, then heirs, heirs of God and fellow heirs with Christ" (Rom. 8:16-17). This process is a divine corrective to the world's distorted notions of patriarchy and hierarchy.

An ancient Christian writer, Dionysius the Areopagite, described hierarchy as something that originates in heaven, where divine light passes through the angels and the saints as if all were transparent.[2] God's gifts, then, are passed from one person to the next, undiluted. Those who are closest

---

[2] Dionysius the Areopagite, *The Celestial Hierarchy*, chap. 13.

to God—and so higher in the hierarchy—serve those who are lower. At each stage, they give as God gives, keeping nothing to themselves.

Notice, here, how spiritual goods differ from material goods. If I have sole ownership of something—say, a sport coat or a tie—someone else can't own it and use it at the same time. The higher goods, however, are spiritual; and spiritual goods—such as faith, hope, love, liturgy, the merits of the saints—can be shared and owned completely by all. That's how the hierarchy works with the angels and saints in heaven.

For this sharing to take place "on earth as it is in heaven" requires the perfection of earthly fatherhood, which can take place only if we earnestly pray, "Our Father who art in heaven." God is the primordial Father, "of whom all paternity in heaven and earth is named" (Eph. 3:15, Douay Rheims Version). He is the eternal model by which all human fathers must be measured.

Why in the Sky?

Down through the ages, skeptics have asked whether praying to "Our Father . . . in heaven" is consistent with our belief that "God is everywhere" and that He dwells within us (cf. Jn. 14:16, 23).

Yes, God is everywhere, on earth as He is in heaven. He is always present with us, and He lives within us when we are in the state of grace, free of mortal sin. Yet Jesus teaches us to pray to "Our Father . . . in heaven" because He wants us to lift our sights from our earthly exile to our true home—in heaven. Saint John Chrysostom said it well: Jesus taught us to pray this way not in order to "limit God to the heavens," but rather to lift us up from earth and set us "in the high places and in the dwellings above."[3]

God made us for Himself; He made us for heaven. Heaven is separated from us not by light-years of space, but by our sins. Yet God Himself created our place of exile, and it's a good place. Thus, it's easy for us to get comfortable in our earthly lives and to forget our eternal destiny. Think of the Israelites wandering in the wilderness; after a few years of hardship, they grew nostalgic for their years of slavery in Egypt, where at least their bellies were full.

We, too, can think that way. When earthly troubles close in on us, heaven's promises seem unreal and remote. When we fix our gaze on the near horizon, envious thoughts, resentments, and greedy impulses seem to make sense to us. After all, if we follow their enticing logic, maybe we can grab hold of the things we want right now.

The remedy to this, of course, is to set our sights on high, to heaven, our promised home. By God's mercy and power—by His fatherhood!—He has promised us great things. Now we live in a state of grace, but then, when we are with "Our Father . . . in heaven," we will live in a state of glory. Now we are His temples; but then He will be *our* Temple (cf. Rev. 21:22). Now, He lives in us; but then, we will live in Him.

Though we're not home yet, God the Father is with us, and He has the power to lead us through the desert and across the Jordan. Though we have a long journey ahead, He is always in our midst.

---

[3] See p. 113.

HALLOWED BE THY NAME

Whenever we pray the Lord's Prayer, we acknowledge God's name as "[h]allowed" (Mt. 6:9)—that is, as *holy* or *sanctified*. But what do we mean by this? Do we mean what Jesus meant?

Most people associate the word *holy* with things that are transcendent—"wholly other," in the defining phrase of the twentieth-century scholar Rudolf Otto.[1] The holy is something entirely different from what we experience in ordinary life. "Holy, holy, holy" is what even the angels cry in the presence of a Power and a Mystery that inspires fear and awe (Is. 6:2-3; cf. Rev. 4:8).

Some scholars suggest that when biblical authors invoke the name of the Lord, rather than the Person of the Lord, they are consciously avoiding any language that might suggest intimacy. They point out that the psalmist says, "Our help is in the name of the LORD, who made heaven and earth" (Ps. 124:8), rather than just, "Our help is in the LORD." Here, they believe that David is verbally distancing himself from a transcendent God.

---

[1] Rudolf Otto, *The Idea of the Holy: An Inquiry into the Non-Rational Factor in the Idea of the Divine and Its Relation to the Rational*, trans. John W. Harvey, 2d ed. (London: Oxford University Press, 1950), 26.

By itself, that idea is half true. God is transcendent, powerful, mysterious, and fearsome. Our God is an awesome God. When we speak of His name as "hallowed," however, we are doing much more than expressing awe, or stating a supernatural fact. This is not the devotional counterpart to a scientist's evocation of "billions and billions" of light-years.

For Jesus' idea of holiness was almost the opposite of Rudolf Otto's. The scholar sees holiness measured in the awe or the fear felt by a believer. Jesus, however, saw holiness as something belonging to God from all eternity, before creation, and so before there was even a single angel or human being to be awestruck by the Almighty.

It's not that Jesus considered God to be anything less than mysterious or powerful; but God's mystery and power were not what made Him holy. "Holy" is His name—that is, His essential identity, independent of whether we exist in order to sense His wonder.

Moreover, what made Him holy was not intended to distance Him from us so much as to draw us near to Him in intimacy.

Blessing or Curse?

The Hebrew word for holiness is *kiddushin*, which also means marriage. When something is holy, it is consecrated, set apart from everything else—in that sense, it is transcendent. Yet it is set apart, not for isolation, but for a personal and interpersonal purpose; not for distance, but for intimacy.

In the ancient world, this consecration was achieved by means of a covenant. More than a contract, more than a treaty, a covenant created a family bond between persons or between nations. A wedding took the form of a covenant oath; so did the adoption of a child or the naming of a newborn. These new family relationships brought with them certain privileges and duties. The parties of a covenant invoked God's name as they swore to fulfill their responsibilities. Should they fail, they accepted the most dire penalties, because they had placed themselves under God's judgment. By entering into a covenant relationship, they were, in effect, calling down a blessing or a curse (cf. Deut. 11:26). If they were faithful, they would receive God's blessing. If they were unfaithful, they drew down their own curse.

God's name itself served as an oath. To invoke His name was to call upon Him and place oneself under His judgment. The name of God is the power behind the covenant.

The name of God, then, is His own covenant identity, His personal identity. It's what proves our personal relationship with Him. When we call upon that name—"Our Father!"—God responds as a Father, and we receive His help. We also bring on His judgment, but that judgment is a blessing to those who avail themselves of His help.

When Jesus teaches us to pray, "Hallowed be thy name" (Mt. 6:9), He shows us that the name of God is consecrated. It is holy. God's name is not merely transcendent and mysterious; it is intimate and personal and interpersonal. It is the basis for the covenant.

The Claim to Name

This is an astounding fact—even more astounding when we consider God as awesome and transcendent. He is all these things, and yet He is ours. He is our Father!

Consider the following passage from Exodus, when God is establishing the terms of His covenant with Israel: "Now therefore, if you will obey my voice and keep my covenant, you shall be my own possession among all peoples; for all the earth is mine" (Ex. 19:5). That seems a paradoxical claim. God first says that Israel is His possession; then He goes on to say that all the world is His. What, then, makes Israel so different?

God was, however, expressing a special relationship with Israel, and He did so by using the word *segullah*, which denoted something set apart, reserved for the use of a king. A king, after all, legally owns all the real estate in his kingdom; but the palace is set apart for his private use. He owns all the jewels in the realm; but the crown jewels are his special possession.

We recognize, then, that we are God's special possession, and God is ours. We are His children and not just His creatures. All creatures possess God as their Beginning and End, but we possess Him as children of the King, children who live in the palace and are heirs to the throne.

God's name is set apart—*segullah*—as the possession of the King of heaven, and of those who are, by covenant, the children of the King. In possessing God, we recognize that His name is holy, consecrated, set apart for intimate conversation within the Family of God.

The Virgin Mary said, "[H]oly is his name" (Lk. 1:49). He is not holy merely in relation to human beings who hold Him in awe. Holy is His name from all eternity, for we invoke Him with the proper name "Holy Spirit." As God's Family on earth, we share in His holiness because we are called by His name and are children of His covenant, which we invoke whenever we say, "Our Father."

This is why we must never (in the words of the commandment) "take the name of the LORD your God in vain" (Ex. 20:7). When we call upon the name of the Lord, we are reminding God of the special relationship He has with us. We do this not for His sake, but for our own. He, after all, does not forget, though we do again and again.

When we call upon God's holy name, we must be prepared to approach Him as "our Father." That means we must place ourselves under judgment, calling down a great blessing or a great curse. For a father asks more from his children than a judge asks from a defendant, a teacher from a pupil, or a boss from an employee.

When we speak of the name of the Lord, we're not getting less of God or putting a greater distance between ourselves and Him. The Lord has revealed His name so that we might call upon His power and draw closer to Him in communion. That's the most awesome mystery we'll ever know.

CHAPTER FOUR

THY KINGDOM COME

If some people find it difficult to identify with God as Father—because of their own troubled relationships with earthly fathers—how much more must they miss the relevance of God as King. If human fathers are a vanishing breed, then human monarchs are practically extinct.

My country is proud that its history began with the overthrow of a king, and that no sovereign has ever ruled our land since then. Many other countries, in Europe for example, have retained monarchs, but only as ceremonial figures with little authority or power. As we grew up, most of us learned about the ancient ideal of kingship, for the most part, from fairy tales.

I dare say we're missing something here. We're missing an idea that beats as the heart of the Gospel. For Jesus came for nothing if not to establish a Kingdom: "The kingdom of heaven is at hand" (Mt. 10:7).

The idea of the Kingdom is obviously important to Jesus and to the sacred writers of the New Testament. In Matthew's Gospel alone, there are almost forty references to the "Kingdom of God" and the "Kingdom of heaven." Throughout the Gospels, Jesus develops the idea, mostly in parables, though sometimes He puts the matter quite plainly: "[T]he kingdom of God is in the midst of you" (Lk. 17:21).

Yet, for us today, the meaning of even these seemingly simple statements can be elusive. In order for us to understand what Jesus meant by "Kingdom," we need to understand what "Kingdom" meant in His language and His nation.

Send in the Crowns

The word "Kingdom" had a concrete historical meaning for the People of Israel. Indeed, the twelve tribes of Israel considered themselves, collectively, to be the "Kingdom of God."

For many centuries, from the Exodus until around 1000 B.C., the tribes lived in the promised land, recognizing no king but Yahweh (cf. Deut. 33:5). That was the theory, at least. The truth, however, is that the people still had something of an inferiority complex, and they wanted their nation to be like other nations, with the same symbols of worldly power. They wanted to have a king, a throne, a royal dynasty. In the Book of Judges, we see that the people clamored to crown the great warrior, Gideon. But Gideon said to them, "I will not rule over you, and my son will not rule over you; the LORD will rule over you" (Judg. 8:23). Still, the cry arose again in another generation: "[A]ppoint for us a king to govern us like all the nations" (1 Sam. 8:5).

God let them have their way—though, in the long run, He was letting them have His way. For the dynasty that would soon establish itself was the line of King David, who was "a man after [God's] own heart" (1 Sam. 13:14); and from the line of David would come a King Who would bring all the nations of the world under the kingship of God. God said to David: "Ask of me, and I will make the nations your heritage" (Ps. 2:8). And David's house would reign not only universally, but everlastingly. That promise was the substance of God's covenant with David: "I will raise up your offspring after you. . . . I will be his father, and he shall be my son. . . . And your house and your kingdom shall be made sure for ever before me; your throne shall be established for ever" (2 Sam. 7:12, 14, 16). Even when the Davidic line was in its apparent downfall—when the lands of the kingdom were shattered by rebellion, and when the people were scattered in exile—even then, Israel's prophets predicted that the kingdom of Israel (and so, the Kingdom of God) would be restored by a righteous descendent of David (cf. Jer. 23:5).

Kingdom by Covenant

The righteous King, the Son of David, the King of Kings would be Jesus Christ. The first words of the New Testament establish Jesus' royal pedigree: "The book of the genealogy of Jesus Christ, the son of David" (Mt. 1:1). Many times He is addressed as "Son of David," even though most Jews considered David's line to have been extinct for centuries.

The evangelists are careful to depict Jesus' Davidic royalty, even from His earliest days. He is born in the city of King David. He is often shown "with Mary his mother" (Mt. 2:11), just as the ancient king of Israel always ruled, not with his (multiple) wives, but beside his mother, the *gebirah* or queen mother.

Thus, the reign of God is not merely His governance over creation. God has always governed the universe, which He created and continues to hold in existence.

No, the Kingdom of God refers, rather, to a specific historical reality: the reign that God established by covenant with David, and which He renewed by Jesus Christ. With the coming of Jesus, "the kingdom of heaven is at hand" (Mt. 3:2). The Kingdom of heaven has come to earth.

Some people recognized this. Nathanael proclaimed Jesus' divine and Davidic kingship upon first meeting Him: "Rabbi, you are the Son of God! You are the King of Israel!" (Jn. 1:49).

Christian tradition goes so far as to identify the Kingdom with Jesus Himself (cf. Catechism, no. 2816). This, however, raises a difficulty: If the Kingdom has come with Jesus Christ, why did Jesus Himself teach us to pray for the coming of the Kingdom? Why should we pray, "Thy kingdom come" (Mt. 6:10)?

Jesus taught His disciples to pray for the Kingdom because, even though the King has come among us, He has not yet manifested Himself fully. Even in Jesus' lifetime, most people did not see His kingship. He did not match their worldly idea of a king. Remember, the Israelites had first wanted a king because they were jealous of the Gentiles, whose kings were symbols of power (cf. 1 Sam. 8:4-5). Pontius Pilate used Jesus' unkingliness as the basis for his interrogation. "My kingship," Jesus replied, "is not of this world" (Jn. 18:36).

His Kingdom has entered the world. It is here. Yet it is not fully manifest. It is present invisibly and veiled sacramentally. In that sense, it is like Jesus Himself, Who possessed all the glory of God, though He revealed this glory through humble, human flesh.

The Royal Road

Jesus promised us a Kingdom, and He kept His promise. When His Father raised Him from the dead, He established through His own resurrected Body (which is the Eucharist) His Mystical Body (which is the Kingdom). He said, "[T]he kingdom of heaven is at hand" (Mt. 3:2). And so it is—it is as near as our local parish. For where the King is present, there is the Kingdom. And where the Eucharist is, there is the King.

"The Kingdom of God has been coming since the Last Supper," says the Catechism, "and, in the Eucharist, it is in our midst" (no. 2816). That's why we pray the Our Father at the climactic moment in the Mass, just before we receive Jesus in Holy Communion. "In the Eucharist, the Lord's Prayer . . . is the proper prayer of 'the end-time,' the time of salvation that began with the outpouring of the Holy Spirit and will be fulfilled with the Lord's return" (Catechism, no. 2771).

The Kingdom is here, and the King is among us. He is here in all His glory, and He reigns in mystery, in the Eucharist, in the Church. Saint Augustine put it plainly: "Now the Church is the Kingdom of Christ and the Kingdom of heaven."[1] Even now, in the Church, Christ rules in all His glory, though we lack the vision to see such glory in its fullness. We walk by faith, for now; but later, God willing, we will walk by sight.

When we pray, "Thy kingdom come," we ask for an ever-increasing manifestation of the glory of Jesus' real

---

[1] [N]unc Ecclesia Regnum Christi est Regnumque caelorum (Saint Augustine, *City of God*, bk. 20, chap. 9).

presence. The Kingdom has come to us: in the past, in the Incarnation; in the present, in the Eucharist; and it will come to us in fullness in the future, in the unveiling of divine glory at Christ's Second Coming.

CHAPTER FIVE

THY WILL BE DONE

We pray, "Thy will be done" (Mt. 6:10), and it flows pretty easily from our lips. But do we really have a choice?

Indeed, we do. God leaves us free. We may choose to accept His will and do His will. Or we may choose to resist. Our resistance, however, brings for us its own pains. For the will of God is inexorable. It's going to be accomplished, no matter how much we push back against it. And just as physical resistance to a mighty force can leave us bruised and brush burned, so our resistance to God's almighty will can leave us weary in spirit, sad, and weak. For God wills our joy, though it may not come easily; and so, to oppose His will is to oppose our own happiness.

Our freedom of choice, then, is a relative sort of freedom. We may choose whom we will serve: God or ourselves. Either way, we can count on a struggle, but only one way leads to happiness.

Why Bother?

Still, it's fair to ask, Why bother to pray, "Thy will be done"? Isn't it presumptuous, or even redundant? Isn't God's will what happens anyway? Why *pray* for God's will? It seems like praying for gravity to continue.

The answer is simple. When we pray, "Thy will be done," we do not change or strengthen the will of God, but we do change and strengthen ourselves. Such prayer disposes our hearts to do the will of the Father (cf. Catechism, no. 2611). Our prayer conditions us to say, "*Thy* will," when the pull of our nature says, "*My* will." In the Garden of Gethsemane, we see Jesus Himself struggling against the natural human instinct for self-preservation, the natural human dread of pain and death. "My Father, if it be possible, let this cup pass from me; nevertheless, not as I will, but as thou wilt" (Mt. 26:39).

Earthly life is good, but we must reach beyond it if we want to reach heaven. Our human will is good, but we must reach beyond it if we want to be divine—if we want to be holy—if we want to be saints. And make no mistake about it: Only saints can live in heaven, only those who say, "Thy will be done." Jesus said, "Not every one who says to me, 'Lord, Lord,' shall enter the kingdom of heaven, but he who does the will of my Father who is in heaven" (Mt. 7:21).

What gets us to heaven is our ability to share in the divine life, to be "partakers of the divine nature" (2 Pet. 1:4). How do mere humans become divine? By sharing in the life of God, Who became human. Jesus Christ—God incarnate, the Word made flesh—established a "new covenant" that enables the communion between us and God to occur (Lk. 22:20). It's important that we understand what Jesus was doing. A covenant is not a business transaction, not a deal, and not a contract. All those things exchange goods and services, but a covenant exchanges *persons.* That's why marriage is a covenant, and so is the adoption of a child. A covenant draws people not into a business partnership, but into a family relationship. Thus, a covenant is a union of wills. I don't lose my will in God's, any more than I lose my will in my wife's. I unite my will to His. In doing so, I begin to live more perfectly in Jesus, the eternal Son of the Father, for He said, "I seek not my own will but the will of him who sent me" (Jn. 5:30). I begin to live more perfectly the life of the Trinity.

The covenant is what makes us part of God's Family, and all covenants require a union of wills. Jesus said: "[W]hoever does the will of my Father in heaven is my brother, and sister, and mother" (Mt. 12:50). As brothers and sisters of Christ, we are, in the words of Tradition, "sons in the Son."

Between the Poles

Thus, what we're praying for is not fatalistic resignation, but to will what He wills, as forcefully as He wills it—with filial boldness.

There are many ways we can misunderstand this petition. Some people look upon it as fatalistic resignation: "Well, God, You're going to do what You want anyway; I'd better just grit my teeth and accept it!" Others find it a source of agonizing scruples and endless, troubled inquiry: They wring their hands and say, "Thy will be done, Lord . . . but how can I ever know Thy will?"—as if they dare not think for themselves in the presence of a Power so mighty. In neither of these do we find the attitude of a child toward his father.

Both fatalism and pietism are, at root, denials of God's fatherhood. They both see God the way a slave sees His master: either with resentment or with servile fear. Yet, between these two extremes we find the attitude that is appropriate: the trusting love of a son for his father. Jesus taught us to pray, "Our Father," so that we may, even now, begin to share in the life of the Trinity. And this is the life of the Trinity: The Father eternally pours Himself out in love for the Son; the Son eternally returns all His love to the Father; and the love they share is the Holy Spirit. When we unite our will with the Father's will, we begin to love as the Father loves and give ourselves as the Father gives—and will as the Father wills.

There is nothing anxious in this attitude. There is no sigh of resignation. This is the deep peace of which Saint Augustine spoke when he summed up the Christian life: "Love, and do what you will."[1] For the child of God, doing God's will should be as natural as eating. Think of Jesus' words: "My food is to do the will of him who sent me" (Jn. 4:34).

Will to Power

I have often thought that this is the reason why Jesus taught us to begin our prayers by invoking God as "Father," rather than with the traditional invocation of God as "Lord" or "King of the Universe." It's not that God's will isn't sovereign, like a king's—surely it is!—but it is, above all, loving and merciful, like a father's.

---

[1] Saint Augustine, *Homily VII on the First Epistle of John,* no. 8.

We begin by praying, "Our Father," but we press on, we persevere, by lovingly accepting and doing the will of God. Again, it is this union of wills that perfects us as children of God. And such a divine relation is, in a sense, exactly what we're praying for when we say, "Thy will be done." For, in the words of Saint Paul, "this is the will of God, your sanctification" (1 Thess. 4:3).

God's will means more for us than merely following the law. The commandments express His will, but they do not exhaust it. His will for us is much greater. It's nothing short of a sharing in His own life, which is the deepest freedom we can know.

ON EARTH
AS IT IS IN HEAVEN

We know we're not in heaven now. Yet we know that heaven is all that matters. So what should we be doing on earth, for heaven's sake?

We should be manifesting God's Kingdom and fulfilling His will as perfectly on earth as the angels do in heaven.

Celestial Voices Impersonated

This idea was not "news" with the Gospel. The people of ancient Israel considered their earthly liturgy to be a divinely inspired imitation of heavenly worship. Both Moses and Solomon constructed God's earthly dwellings—the tabernacle and the Temple—according to a heavenly archetype revealed by God Himself (cf. Ex. 25:8-27:21; 1 Chron. 28:19; Wis. 9:8). The prophets expressed this belief in a mystical way, as they depicted the angels worshiping amid songs and trappings that were clearly recognizable from the Jerusalem Temple (cf. Is. 6:1-7; Ezek. 1:4-28). The hymns sung by the angels were the same songs the Levites sang before the earthly sanctuary.

We find the idea in full flower at the time of Jesus Christ and expressed in the apocryphal books of Enoch and Jubilees and in the recently discovered Dead Sea

Scrolls.[1] What the priests did in the Temple sanctuary was an earthly imitation of what the angels did in heaven.

And none of this was mere pageantry. Both the heavenly and earthly liturgies had more than a ceremonial purpose. The angelic liturgy preserved a certain order not only in the courts of the Almighty, but also in the entire universe. God had given over the governance of creation to His angels, and so the world itself was caught up in a cosmic liturgy: "Holy, holy, holy is the LORD of hosts; the whole earth is full of his glory" (Is. 6:3; cf. Rev. 4:8). As Israel's priests performed their Temple liturgy, they—like their counterparts in heaven—preserved and sanctified the order of the cosmos.

Thus, Israel's worship overflowed to form Israel's culture. This is what made David a man after God's own heart. He wanted to configure earthly space and time so that all of the kingdom's temporal works flowed from worship and returned to God as a sacrifice of praise and thanksgiving. He moved the ark of the covenant to rest at the center of his capital city, and he planned a magnificent temple as its home. He endowed the priests and their attendants richly, and he himself composed beautiful liturgies for their use. His successor son, Solomon, followed suit (cf. 2 Chron. 1-7).

The Big Breakthrough

With all of that in their cultural and historical background, the Jews of Jesus' time would have recognized

---

[1] Cf. Carol Newsom, ed., *Songs of the Sabbath Sacrifice: A Critical Edition* (Atlanta, Ga.: Scholar Press, 1985).

the beauty of His petition, "Thy will be done, [o]n earth as it is in heaven" (Mt. 6:10), in a way that many of us today do not.

To the ancient People of God, heaven and earth were distinct, but earth traced the motions of heaven most clearly in the rites of the Temple. They recognized that to worship God in this way was an awesome gift. Yet it was still only a shadow of the angels' worship—and only a shadow of the earthly worship that would be inaugurated by Jesus Christ.

By assuming human flesh, Jesus brought heaven to earth. Moreover, with His very flesh, He has fulfilled and perfected the worship of ancient Israel. No longer must the People of God worship in imitation of angels. In the liturgy of the New Covenant, the renewed Israel—the Church—worships *together with the angels*. In the New Testament, the Book of Revelation shows us the *shared* liturgy of heaven and earth. Around the throne of God, men and angels bow down and worship together (cf. Rev. 5:14); an angel lifts the seer up to stand beside him (cf. Rev. 19:10). Moreover, the renewed Israel is a nation of priests (cf. Rev. 5:10; 20:6), so that all are admitted to the holiest inner sanctum of the Temple. It's no wonder that Eastern writers say that the Book of Revelation is an "icon of the liturgy."[2]

Christ has broken down all the barriers—between man and angel, Jew and Gentile, priest and people. In

---

[2] Cf. G. A. Gray, "The Apocalypse of Saint John the Theologian: Verbal Icon of Liturgy" (master's thesis, Mount Angel Seminary, 1989).

the worship of the New Covenant, Christ Himself presides, and we not only imitate the angels—we participate with them.

Today, we know this worship as the Mass. There, Christ Himself presides as High Priest. The liturgy is the manifestation in time of His perfect offering in eternity.

Saint John Chrysostom spoke of this mystery in the most dazzling terms, all of them drawn from the Book of Revelation:

> What are the heavenly things he speaks of here [in Hebrews 10]? The spiritual things. For although they are done on earth, yet nevertheless they are worthy of the [h]eavens. For when our Lord Jesus Christ lies slain (as a sacrifice), when the Spirit is with us, when He who sitteth on the right hand of the Father is here, when sons are made sons by the [w]ashing, when they are fellow-citizens of those in [h]eaven, when we have a country, and a city, and citizenship there, when we are strangers to things here, how can all these be other than "heavenly things"? But what! Are not our [h]ymns heavenly? Do not we also who are below utter in concert with them the same things which the divine choirs of bodiless powers sing above? Is not the altar also heavenly?[3]

Making History

Once again, though, we have to be very clear. This is not mere ceremonial of the royal court. This is the cosmic

---

[3] Saint John Chrysostom, *Homily XIV on the Epistle to the Hebrews*, in *Nicene and Post-Nicene Fathers*, 1st ser., vol. 14, ed. Philip Schaff (Peabody, Mass.: Hendrickson Publishers, 1994), 434.

liturgy, perfected for the children of God who reign in Christ. Since the coming of Christ, the heavenly-earthly liturgy is the instrument par excellence of God's will; it is the fullest manifestation of His Kingdom. Nowhere else is our prayer so richly fulfilled: "Thy kingdom come, Thy will be done, on earth as it is in heaven." We see, in Revelation, that when the angels and the saints present their prayers to Almighty God, the earth quakes and thunder peals, and the angelic powers unleash war, economic depression, famine, and death upon the earth.

W. H. Auden was famous for saying that "poetry makes nothing happen."[4] If that's so, then liturgy is certainly not what he'd call poetry. For John the seer, the author of Revelation, shows us that the prayers of the Church—of the living, the dead, and the angels—direct not only the course of history, but the phenomena of nature as well.

All of that is what takes place when we go to Mass. There, the power of God works through His angels and His saints, who are His adopted children—and that means you and me.

---

[4] "In Memory of W. B. Yeats," in *The Collected Poetry of W. H. Auden* (New York: Random House, 1945), 50.

CHAPTER SEVEN

GIVE US THIS DAY OUR DAILY BREAD

There's something childlike about the turn we take with the fourth petition of the Lord's Prayer. In the first three petitions, we prayed to God for the sake of His name, His will, His Kingdom.

Now we turn, like children, to ask Him for "our" bread. It is interesting to note that we ask Him for food as if it already belonged to us—as if He had an obligation to provide it—as if He were our Father.

Bread for Greatness

This is the filial boldness of God's children. We ask, and we know we shall receive. For what father, "if his son asks him for bread, will give him a stone?" (Mt. 7:9).

We ask for *our* bread because we address *our* Father, and fathers produce families, not individuals.

It's interesting, too, that we ask for "our" bread and not "my" bread. Jesus teaches us that even when we pray in private (cf. Mt. 6:6), we do not pray alone. We pray in solidarity with all the children of God, the Church of the living and the saints in heaven. And we pray *for* the whole Church, that all may have the bread they need today. This prayer is something intimate, yet something shared. It's familial.

In the ancient world, the dispensation of daily bread was a sign of a kingdom's prosperity. When the nation was doing well, winning its wars, and selling its goods, its citizens received an ample ration of bread, "without money and without price" (Is. 55:1). Even greater was Israel's vision of the ongoing banquet that would come with the reign of the anointed Son of David, the Messiah (cf. Is. 65:13-14).

The first Christians recognized that the Son of David had begun His reign—and His banquet. Moreover, His banquet had spiritual benefits that surpassed the most sumptuous worldly feast. For all the early Christian commentators, "our bread" meant not only their everyday material needs, but also their need for communion with God. "Our bread," in common speech, meant the Eucharist. "[T]hey devoted themselves to the apostles' teaching and fellowship, to the breaking of bread and the prayers. . . . And day by day, attending the temple together and breaking bread in their homes" (Acts 2:42, 46).

In the generations after the death of the apostles, we find that the common practice of Christians was to receive the Eucharist every day. Tertullian attests to this in North Africa, and Saint Hippolytus in Rome.[1] Saint Cyprian of Carthage, in 252, speaks at length about the spiritual meaning of this petition: "And as we say, 'Our Father,' because He is the Father of those who understand and believe, so also we call it 'our bread,' because Christ is the Bread of those who are in union with His Body. And we

---

[1] Tertullian, *Ad Uxorem* (To His Wife), bk. 2, chap. 5; *The Apostolic Tradition of Saint Hippolytus*, ed. Gregory Dix (London: SPCK, 1937), 58.

ask that this Bread be given to us daily, that we who are in Christ and daily receive the Eucharist for the food of salvation may not, by the interposition of some heinous sin, be prevented from receiving Communion and from partaking of the heavenly Bread and be separated from Christ's Body."[2]

That Says It All

How succinctly this petition expresses all our needs in life, both individual and corporate, both material and spiritual. Saint Augustine said that there are three levels of meaning to the bread we ask for: (1) all those things that meet the wants of this life; (2) the Sacrament of the Body of Christ, which we may daily receive; and (3) our spiritual Food, the Bread of life, Who is Jesus.[3]

Our bodies hunger after food; our souls hunger after God. God will fulfill both hungers because He is our Father. He can fulfill both hungers because He is almighty—"Our Father . . . in heaven." We pray to the God who loves us so much that He has counted the hairs of our heads (cf. Lk. 12:7). This is the God who can "spread a table in the wilderness" (Ps. 78:19), the God who drew water from a dry desert rock.

A child trusts his father to provide for his needs as they arise. A little child has no clear concept of the future, and so has little worry about tomorrow. The Lord's Prayer teaches us to desire a child's life of humility, trust, and dependence on God. We ask not for riches, but only for

---

[2] See pp. 92-93.
[3] See pp. 143-44.

what we need for the day. We are confident that God will provide. This is a valuable lesson for us grown-ups to learn. We pride ourselves on self-reliance; we tend to want to control our lives and the lives of others. But, says Saint Augustine, "no matter how rich a man is on earth, he is still God's beggar."[4]

Praying this way, we cultivate "a saintlike poverty," says Saint Cyril of Alexandria. "For to ask is not the part of those who have, but of those rather who are in need . . . and cannot do without."[5]

Unsolved Mysteries

One word of this petition has baffled both scholars and saints since the early days of the Church. It is the word *epioúsios*, which we usually translate as "daily." Some English translations have us pray for our "daily bread"; others, for our "bread for tomorrow"; still others, for our "supersubstantial bread." The truth is that the word is impossible to translate, since it appears nowhere else in all of ancient Greek literature; nor does it appear in personal correspondence, legal documents, or business records that have survived from the time of Christ. The greatest Fathers of the Church wrestled with the mystery— Cyril of Alexandria and Jerome are among the giants who have left us studies—and admitted the possibility of all

---

[4] Saint Augustine, *Sermon VI on New Testament Lessons*, in *Nicene and Post-Nicene Fathers*, 1st ser., vol. 6, ed. Philip Schaff (Peabody, Mass.: Hendrickson Publishers, 1994), 276.
[5] Saint Cyril of Alexandria, *Homily 75*, in *Commentary on the Gospel of St. Luke* (n.p.: Studion Publishers, 1983).

the modern readings. But they could come to no final agreement about *epioúsios*.

Tradition, however, leaves us with a solution: It's all true. We pray for our daily bread, for the material needs of the day. We pray for our daily spiritual communion with Jesus. We pray that God will give us grace in super-abundance. And we pray even today for our "bread for tomorrow"—our share, right now, in the heavenly banquet of Jesus Christ, every time we go to Mass.

FORGIVE US ...
AS WE FORGIVE

The Our Father is a prayer of limitless depth. Taken all at once, it can be overwhelming. So it's good for us to take the time, as we have been doing, to meditate upon each of the prayer's petitions individually.

We must, however, avoid the temptation to look at each petition as if it were thematically separate from the others. There is a unity to the Lord's Prayer, and its petitions follow a certain logical progression. We can see this most vividly as we move from "[g]ive us this day our daily bread" (Mt. 6:11) to "forgive us our trespasses" (cf. Mt. 6:12).

It is no accident that Jesus paired these petitions in a single sentence. There is a logical link between "our daily bread" and our forgiveness. For among the chief effects of the "daily bread" Christ has given us in Holy Communion is the complete remission of all our venial sins.

The Mass is a sacrifice, and so the "daily bread" is a daily offering for sin, like those prefigured in the Temple of ancient Israel. Saint Justin Martyr spelled this out clearly, around A.D. 150, in language that echoes the Lord's Prayer. Israel's offering of fine flour, he wrote, "which was prescribed to be presented on behalf of those purified from leprosy, was a type of the bread of the Eucharist, the celebration of which our Lord Jesus Christ prescribed, in remembrance of the suffering which He endured on behalf of those who are purified in soul from all iniquity, in order that we may at the same time thank God . . . for delivering us from the evil."[1]

As Above, So Below

Our bodies long for food; our souls long for God, and this Bread is both food and God. Thus, It meets the needs of both the bodies and the souls of God's children. How does this happen? The Catechism gives us insight: "As bodily nourishment restores lost strength, so the Eucharist strengthens our charity, which tends to be weakened in daily life; and this living charity *wipes away venial sins*" (no. 1394, emphasis in original).

This is more than a mere absolving of debts. This "living charity" is the gift of God's life. In Holy Communion, we are made holy because we are "partakers of the divine nature" (2 Pet. 1:4). For holiness is not just obedience. Only God is holy. Any holiness we have, we have through the life we share in communion with the Trinity. Jesus Himself quoted the psalm: "[Y]ou are gods" (Jn. 10:34; cf. Ps. 82:6)! This divine life we could never achieve on our own; we can only receive it as a gift from God. "You shall be holy, for I am holy" (1 Pet. 1:16; cf. Lev. 11:44-45).

Sin is incompatible with this life, this holiness, this living charity. We cannot live the life of the Trinity, as "sons in the Son," unless we become sinless as He is sinless. Said Saint John Chrysostom: "[T]o call God 'Father' is the pro-

---

[1] Saint Justin Martyr, *Dialogue with Trypho*, in *Ante-Nicene Fathers*, vol. 1, ed. Alexander Roberts and James Donaldson (Peabody, Mass.: Hendrickson Publishers, 1994), 215.

fession of a blameless life."[2] Thus, when grace encounters sin in our souls, something has to give way. The grace of our "daily bread" takes out our sin from above.

Our Lord would have us take out sin from below as well. Thus, He teaches us to place a condition on God's forgiveness: "[F]orgive us . . . as we forgive those who trespass against us" (cf. Mt. 6:12). We must not pray too quickly here; it's all too easy for us to miss the sheer impossibility of this condition. For, as we read in the Gospel, "[w]ho can forgive sins but God alone?" (Mk. 2:7). Forgiveness is an action that is purely divine.

Jesus is asking us here to live the divine life that we have received. "[A]s he who called you is holy, be holy yourselves" (1 Pet. 1:15). To forgive is what it means to be divinized. We're not just forgiving because we believe our offenders' apologies are sincere, and they won't trouble us again—because sometimes they're not sincere, sometimes they don't even bother to say they're sorry, and often they sin against us again and again. But God forgives us when we apologize halfheartedly and when we become repeat offenders.

So we forgive as God forgives, in imitation not only of the quantity but also the quality of His forgiveness. Like God, we forgive, not merely by forgetting, but by loving. It is the heat of God's love that melts the ice of our sin; and so it is the heat of our love that will bring about the forgiveness of those who trespass against us. We don't just remit their debts; we love our enemies into wholeness, as

---

[2] See p. 118.

God has loved us into wholeness. We melt their cold hearts, the ice of their sin. Such forgiveness is an action purely divine, even when it's done by humans. Such forgiveness is possible only by humans who are being divinized.

We forgive as we've been forgiven. We forgive as God forgives. Only then should we ask God to forgive us as we forgive others.

This is how we take out sin from below: by extending the divine life we have received from above.

Sin Happens

This petition of the Lord's Prayer helps us to acquire the right attitude about ourselves and our fallen humanity, our need for forgiveness, and our potential for divinization.

Sin is something that afflicts all of us. We all sin; we are all the victims of the sins of others. Adam, the original sinner, was himself sinned against by the serpent. The Scriptures tell us that even the just man falls seven times a day (cf. Prov. 24:16).

By placing a plea for forgiveness on our lips, the Lord's Prayer humbles us and forces us to confront a truth that we'd rather avoid. For it can be as difficult for us to notice our own sins as it is easy for us to see the sins of others. Our own faults are trifling (or so we like to think), but others' faults are glaring. "Why," asked Jesus, "do you see the speck that is in your brother's eye, but do not notice the log that is in your own eye?" (Mt. 7:3)

We cannot pray the Our Father honestly without acknowledging the logs in our own eyes—and promising to overlook the specks in our brother's eye. We should make excuses for the faults of others at least as much as we do for our own faults.

To err is human—that is certainly true—but to forgive is divine. When we forgive, we act as God acts. We forgive others as we have been forgiven first.

LEAD US NOT INTO TEMPTATION ...

The Lord's Prayer is like a marathon course whose last mile winds up a steep hill. Or it's like a Himalayan mountain whose ultimate peak crowns a sheer, vertical rock face.

We approach the end of the Our Father, and still we face the petition that has proven a stumbling block to many great minds in Christian history. The psychoanalyst C. G. Jung's misinterpretation of this petition was a major factor in his break with orthodox Christianity. He cited Jesus' words as evidence that God is not merely "love and goodness," but also "the tempter and destroyer."[1]

Why, after all, would God lead us into temptation? When the Scriptures speak of a "tempter," they always mean the Devil (cf. Mt. 4:3; 1 Thess. 3:5). Temptation is the hallmark of Satan's action in our lives. Why, then, are we praying that God—"Our Father . . . in heaven"—will not lead us into temptation?

God Does Not Tempt

We must read Jesus' words with utmost care, for He chose them with a precision that is perfect and all-knowing.

---

[1] C. G. Jung, *Memories, Dreams, Reflections*, ed. Aniela Jaffé, trans. Richard and Clara Winston (New York: Pantheon Books, 1963), 56.

The Lord's Prayer is not the only time Jesus directed His followers to pray against temptation. Twice in the Garden of Gethsemane, He urged the apostles, "Pray that you may not enter into temptation. . . . Rise and pray that you may not enter into temptation" (Lk. 22:40, 46).

We may conclude, then, that temptations are something to be strenuously avoided. However, Jesus also said that temptations are inevitable: "For it is necessary that temptations come, but woe to the man by whom the temptation comes!" (Mt. 18:7). It is clear, in this last context, that God is not the originator of temptations. God does not tempt us. "Let no one say when he is tempted, 'I am tempted by God'; for God cannot be tempted with evil and he himself tempts no one" (Jas. 1:13). But temptations do come—from our fellowmen, as Jesus implies above; from the Devil, as we see in Jesus' encounter with Satan in the desert (cf. Mt. 4:1-11); and from adverse circumstances in life, such as physical illness, failure, or humiliation.

God does not will our pain; nor does He will the sins of others, which cause us pain. Suffering and death came into the world as a result of the sin of Adam and Eve. Yet God's will is accomplished in spite of these things; and He has ordained every occasion of temptation to be an occasion of grace as well. It all turns on how we respond.

Freedom's Guarantee

This is a subtle matter, but a very important one, and it is easy to see how it has scandalized even great minds such as Jung's—for it involves the cooperation of God's omnipotent will and our human freedom.

God did not force Adam and Eve to love or obey Him. He allowed them a choice. He placed them in a garden full of delights and invited them to partake of any tree but one. "[O]f the tree of the knowledge of good and evil you shall not eat," God commanded, "for in the day that you eat of it you shall die" (Gen. 2:17).

Temptation came to the primal couple in the form of a serpent—a deadly beast with an angelic intelligence. He posed veiled threats as, with crafty words, he undermined Adam and Eve's trust in God. Fearing for their lives, and too proud to cry out for help, they consented to the temptation. They sinned, and in sinning they failed the test that God had permitted for their good. If they had feared God more than they feared the serpent, they would have chosen martyrdom at that moment, and they would have entered into a life even greater than paradise. By offering a complete sacrifice of their lives, they would have begun to live the life of glory. For God is love, and love demands a total gift of self. In eternity, the complete gift of self is the Trinity's inner life. In time, the image of divine life is *sacrificial, life-giving* love. We must die to ourselves for the sake of another. And that's what Adam and Eve failed to do.[2]

Why would God allow this? The Catechism quotes the ancient scholar Origen in this regard: "God does not want to impose the good, but wants free beings" (no. 2847). God

---

[2] See my *A Father Who Keeps His Promises: God's Covenant Love in Scripture* (Ann Arbor, Mich.: Charis Books, 1998), chap. 3, and *First Comes Love: Finding Your Family in the Church and the Trinity* (New York: Doubleday, 2002), chap. 6.

made man and woman to be free. That free choice is what made temptation possible. But it is also what made love possible. For love cannot be coerced; love requires a free movement of the will. With freedom came the potential for the highest love, but also for the gravest peril.

What's the Use?

Origen says that "[t]here is a certain usefulness to temptation" (quoted in Catechism, no. 2847). Temptation, when resisted, strengthens the believer. Indeed, God permits trials for this reason. Temptation makes us face the stark choice: for God or against God. When we make the decision for God, we grow stronger in faith, hope, and love.

Contrary to popular belief, then, temptation is not a sign of God's disfavor or punishment. Indeed, down through history, all of God's "favorites" were led to be tempted by severe trials. Consider Abraham, who was asked to sacrifice his only son. Consider Joseph, who was beaten and sold into slavery by his own brothers. Consider Job, whose family and property perished in Satan's murderous rampage. Above all, consider Jesus, for God did not spare Him the most severe temptations. "Then Jesus *was led up by the Spirit* into the wilderness to be tempted by the devil" (Mt. 4:1, emphasis added). The Greek verb for "lead" is different here from the verb in the Lord's Prayer, but the idea is more emphatic. When Mark tells the same story, he says that "[t]he Spirit immediately drove [Jesus] out into the wilderness" (Mk. 1:12). The Greek verb translated as "drove" means, literally, "threw"! If Jesus Himself was "thrown" into severe temptation, we should not complain that we are unloved by God when He "leads" us into temptation. For, like God's other beloved, we will shine more brightly when we, with God's help, have struggled successfully.

"God tested them and found them worthy of himself; like gold in the furnace he tried them, and like a sacrificial burnt offering he accepted them. In the time of their visitation they will shine forth" (Wis. 3:5-7).

Temptation, then, is something useful in God's providence, because of God's grace.

Tempted to Be Tempted?

Trials are useful, but still we should not seek them out. In fact, we should avoid them as much as we can. Note that Jesus did *not* teach us to pray, "Lead us into temptation." For that would surely be presumptuous of our own power of endurance.

Adam learned the hard way that, on our own, we do not have the strength to overcome temptation. Those who think they can prevail are usually in for a fall, as Adam was.

For who among us is better prepared than were Jesus' apostles? They enjoyed a privileged schooling, at the feet of the Master Himself. They received the Eucharist from Jesus' own hand. Moreover, on that very night, just hours after their First Communion, our Lord warned them in no uncertain terms—twice!—that they were about to face their most fearsome temptation. Yet, like Adam, they failed. They feared. They fled their Master's side. Will our faith stand better under fire?

This is why Jesus urged the apostles to "[p]ray that you may not enter into temptation" (Lk. 22:40, 46). Temptations may be inevitable, but a realistic Christian knows he's not ready for them.

The inner logic of the Our Father should tell us so. To the extent that we don't advance the Kingdom of God, to the extent that we don't do God's will, to the extent that we don't worthily and gratefully receive our daily bread, to the extent that we don't seek forgiveness, to the extent that we don't forgive—to that same extent will we be vulnerable to temptation.

Trial is necessary, but if we enter trial with unforgiven sin or with an unforgiving spirit, we will be unprepared. We'll lose. What is it that causes a difficulty to become a temptation? It is our own inability to bear it—because we have failed to live out the other petitions of the Lord's Prayer.[3]

---

[3] See pp. 137-38.

TEMPTATION, PART II

Though we often pray, "Lead us not into temptation," we know that temptations are inevitable. Moreover, we know that God permits these trials for our good. In the last chapter, we saw that temptations serve to refine us, "like gold in the furnace" (Wis. 3:6). Now, we'll examine how that works.

It's fair for us to ask, after all, why God leads us to face such severe trials. If He wants to know the strength of our faith, He doesn't need to test us to measure it. He knows everything. He knows how weak we are. So temptations don't uncover anything for Him. He doesn't learn anything through the process of our trials.

We, however, have much to learn about ourselves—especially in the area of our most besetting sins. For we're only too willing to overlook our own faults, weaknesses, and habits of sin. Pride and vanity blind us to all but our virtues and earthly accomplishments, feeble as they are.

But our trials often turn out to be our most teachable moments. They're the times when we most keenly sense our weakness and need. In fact, we usually discover our deepest need through our weakness. If we don't feel pain acutely, we don't have the sense to cry out for a doctor. Until we feel hunger intensely, we probably won't go begging for food. Our times of trial are the times when we know our inadequacy, and we're most likely to call upon our Father God.

In his First Letter to the Corinthians (10:12-16), Saint Paul tells us, in four steps, how temptation works to a Christian's advantage.

1. "[L]et any one who thinks that he stands take heed lest he fall." Paul begins by pointing out our weakness and our need for humility. Remember Saint Peter's bluster: "Lord, I am ready to go with you to prison and to death" (Lk. 22:33). He thought he was strong; but, within a few hours, he would commit the most cowardly denial of his Master—three times! He thought he would stand tall, and instead he fell hard. He would have been better off praying that God spare him the temptation.

2. "No temptation has overtaken you that is not common to man." Paul says this not to minimize our pain, but to give us comfort. We should take heart, because others have faced our trials (and worse) and persevered. The history of God's dealings with the saints is full of good, practical examples we can follow, in prayer, in patience, and in acting courageously.

3. "God is faithful," Paul says, "and he will not let you be tempted beyond your strength, but with the temptation will also provide the way of escape, that you may be able to endure it." This promise should give us great hope. For nobody can make it through life's "common" temptations, at least not without God's help. But the good news is that God will never abandon us, and He is greater than any power that afflicts us. Even if Satan himself should attack us, we will prevail if we remain faithful. Saint Cyprian said, "[T]he Adversary can do nothing against

us unless God has previously permitted it."[1] God knows the limits of our strength, and He is always willing to share His own omnipotence, so that we can endure even the most severe trials without sinning.

4. "Therefore, my beloved, shun the worship of idols. . . . The cup of blessing which we bless, is it not a participation in the blood of Christ? The bread which we break, is it not a participation in the body of Christ?" Ah, there it is, our "way of escape," and it is nothing less than "our daily bread." Paul demonstrates that the Eucharist is our help and our hope, because it is our communion with the Flesh and Blood of the God-man. Through the Sacrament, we grow strong with a godlike strength. And what are the idols we must shun? Idols are the things we think will get us through the trials, though they never can. They're the things of this world— sometimes very good things—that we've come to place before God in our lives. Idols make temptations necessary for us. For temptations serve to wean us from our dependence on anything less than God. Nothing less than God can really save us. What's the opposite of idolatry? It's Eucharistic dependence, our holy need for all of God. The temptations that we face are meant to humble us and make us depend on God to the utmost.

That's why "lead us not into temptation" is the prayer of a Christian with a healthful sense of reality. It's a good prayer for weaklings—like you and me—who know their strength, and know God's.[2]

---

[1] See p. 98.
[2] See p. 141.

CHAPTER ELEVEN

DELIVER US FROM EVIL

"Deliver us from evil" is a somewhat misleading translation. In the Greek of the New Testament, there is a definite article before the word *evil*. So Jesus actually commanded us to pray for deliverance from "*the* evil" or, more precisely, "the evil one."

It makes a difference, and a rather large one at that. For there is only one evil, and that is sin. I don't mean to be dismissive of other sufferings—loneliness, rejection, grief, cancer, physical debility, mental illness. These can be horrific trials. But they cannot defeat us if we remain strong with God's own strength. Even if disease or murderers should take our lives, we will not die—indeed, we will never die—as long as we keep faith.

The only real danger, the only reality that deserves the name death, is evil. The only thing we really need to be delivered from is not trial, temptation, suffering, or the grave. The only real enemy is sin.

The Futile System

All sin traces its ancestry to the sin of Satan, the fallen prince of angels. Before Adam and Eve faced him in the garden, he had already made his vain refusal to serve God, enticing a third of heaven's angels to follow him in rebellion. Ever after, he has raged in vain warfare against

God and all His works. He tempted our first parents and so cooperated in bringing the curse of death upon the world. Till now, he has never ceased perpetrating lies and murder against God's children. "Your adversary the devil prowls around like a roaring lion, seeking some one to devour" (1 Pet. 5:8).

The Devil lives to oppose God's will. He tempts us at every turn so that we might follow him in rebellion. For God does not will that anyone should ever sin. We don't have to look long or far to see that the Devil succeeds often in temptation. Perhaps he also succeeds often in the final devouring of souls.

Yet his work is perpetually futile. For God is omnipotent, and so His will is inexorable. God's plan will be accomplished. Almighty God, says Saint Augustine, "would never allow any evil whatsoever to exist in his works if he were not so all-powerful and good as to cause good to emerge from evil itself."[1] Even the greatest evil in history, the torture and murder of God's only Son, "brought the greatest of goods: the glorification of Christ and our redemption" (Catechism, no. 312). In the words of Saint Paul, "where sin increased, grace abounded all the more" (Rom. 5:20).

Thus, the Devil's works are worse than futile. They are self-defeating. For when we struggle against his temptations, we grow stronger in virtue, and we gain divine life through grace. Even if we succumb to his empty

---

[1] Saint Augustine, *Enchiridion on Faith, Hope, and Love*, chap. 3, no. 11, quoted in Catechism, no. 311.

promises, but then return to God in sorrow, we grow stronger still. As long as we remain united to Christ, we need fear nothing from our trials. For they can only work to our benefit.

Pope John Paul II summed it up well in his August 20, 1986, general audience. Satan, he said, "cannot block the construction of the Kingdom of God. . . . Indeed, we can say with St. Paul that the work of the evil one cooperates for the good (cf. Rom. 8:28) and that it helps to build up the glory of the 'chosen' ones (cf. 2 Tim. 2:10)."

The Scriptures give us proof positive in the Book of Job. The Devil afflicts Job with disease and poverty, and he brutally takes the lives of Job's children and his livestock. But Job remains steadfast in his faith in God's goodness. Through the ordeal, Job grows in wisdom, and he proves his love for God when such love seems, by a purely human standard, most difficult to give.

In the end, Job is holier, wiser, and even richer than he had ever been before; and so he is happier. Who gets the credit? Should we give the Devil his due? Except for God Almighty, no one worked harder to bring holiness to Job than did the Devil, and no one wanted it less.

The Best Policy

The "evil one" works no differently in your life than in Job's. No one is working harder for your holiness than the Devil, but no one wants it less. His work in an individual life is always a gamble. If he succeeds in tempting us to despair or to commit other mortal sins, we consent to our own true death, the death of our soul. But if we, like Job (and more, like Jesus), cling to "Our Father . . . in heaven"—rejecting

Satan and all his works and all his pomps—we, too, will be holier, wiser, and richer in the end.

Again, this does not mean we should seek to do individual combat with the Devil. He is an angel of the highest order, with an intelligence that is far superior to the combined intelligence of all humanity. On our own, we do not have the strength to defeat him, and indeed he has been the downfall of many exalted minds and souls throughout history.

We pray for deliverance from Satan because we know that we cannot defeat him in a game of one-on-one; nor do we trust the weakness of our faith. We gladly pray the prayer of realists, the prayer of weaklings; for that is what we are. "Lead us not into temptation, but deliver us from evil." Amen!

Saint Cyprian points out that these petitions are comprehensive insurance policies, providing coverage against every moral and physical evil. "When we have once asked for God's protection against evil and have obtained it, then we stand secure and safe against everything which the Devil and the world work against us. For what fear does a man have in this life, if his guardian in this life is God?"[2]

And He is not merely our Guardian, but our Father.

---

[2] See p. 100.

CHAPTER TWELVE

THE KINGDOM, THE POWER, AND THE GLORY

The Our Father is a prayer full of hope. Indeed, it is so hopeful as to sound audacious. The Mass of Pope Paul VI introduces the Lord's Prayer with these words in Latin: *Praeceptis salutaribus moniti, et divina institutione formati, audemus dicere*—literally, "admonished by saving precepts, and formed by divine instruction, we dare to say . . ."

The official English translation is simpler, but also beautiful: "Let us pray *with confidence* to the Father in the words our Savior gave us" (emphasis added).

Our prayer is confident and daring because our hope is supernatural, surpassing anything that might limit our expectation of fulfillment. God is almighty, so He can deliver. God is our loving Father, so He wants to show us His love. We approach Him with confidence. We speak to Him with the fearlessness of small children before their daddy.

To the unbeliever, or the wavering believer, such hope will surely seem too bold, too ambitious. Yet we must understand it as the very foundation of our Christian life, our spirituality. We are children at play in the courts of our Father, the mighty King. We are, in the traditional formula, "sons in the Son." We share in the life of the Trinity. We are God's children.

If divine filiation is the stuff of our life in Christ, then hope is the substance of the Good News we have to tell the world. "Always be prepared," says Saint Peter, "to make a defense to any one who calls you to account for the hope that is in you" (1 Pet. 3:15).

What is the reason for our hope—our confidence, our audacity?

A "Because" for Our "Why"

The most ancient liturgical texts of the Lord's Prayer make the reasons clear in a prayerful postscript that the Church calls the doxology (literally, "word of glory").

Why do we dare to pray the Our Father?

The answer begins with the word *for*, a conjunction that means "because" or "since."

"For the kingdom, the power, and the glory are yours now and forever" (Mt. 6:13).[1]

Most Catholics in the West know this doxology from the Mass, and also from the devotional prayer of Protestants. When most Protestants pray the Lord's Prayer, they include the doxology.

The doxology is missing from the earliest manuscripts of the New Testament. We find it, however, appended to the Our Father in almost all the ancient liturgies, dating back to the time of the apostles. It appears, for example, in the *Didache* (*The Teaching of the Twelve Apostles*), a manual of instruction which many scholars believe was written in Antioch in A.D. 60-90.

---

[1] Alternative reading in footnote *n* of RSVCE.

It is significant that the doxology, though absent from Scripture, is omnipresent in the Mass of the ancient Church. For the Mass sums up the reasons for the hope of Christians, then and now.

Why do we pray with confidence? Because we know God is almighty.

We can pray that His name will be holy because we know that His name is holy from all eternity.

We can pray for the coming of His Kingdom because we know that His Kingdom is already here.

We can pray with assurance that His will be done because we know His will is inexorable, in spite of our free choices against Him.

You Call This a Kingdom?

To those who lack faith, all of this will seem absurd. The mocking cry of the critic has always been, "Jesus promised you a Kingdom, but all He left you was the Church."

But few people recognized the Son of God when He came incarnate as Jesus of Nazareth. Why should we expect them to notice Him today, when He reigns as King of Kings and Lord of Lords?

Jesus promised His first disciples He would return within their lifetime, and that He would then reign gloriously on the earth. He kept that promise, as He keeps all His promises, though we lack the vision to see their fulfillment.

He promised us a glorious Kingdom within His own generation—and we boldly proclaim that He made good on that promise. For all time, He has established His Eucharistic Kingdom, the Church.

We know, however, that the Kingdom doesn't always *appear* so glorious. Jesus never said it would be paradise. His parables speak instead of wheat growing alongside weeds, and of dragnets taking in both holy mackerel and unholy muck. Only at the end of time will we have the vision to see "the kingdom, the power, and the glory" as they have been from all eternity.

But our Lord promised us a Kingdom now—and He left us the Church! There's no contradiction, no unfulfilled promise. What Jesus promised and what He delivered are one and the same. He said the Kingdom is near, and it is. It's as near as your local parish.

The Kingdom comes where the King is present. Where the Eucharist is, there is the King. The "kingdom, the power, and the glory" are already here on earth, because the Church, the Eucharistic Kingdom, is already in heaven.

Forever and ever. Amen!

LAST WORDS

Prayer is necessary, but it's not easy. "[F]or we do not know how to pray as we ought" (Rom 8:26). We know how to pray in a superficial way, but not as we ought. The good news is that our Father knows this, and so He has sent His Son to teach us and has sent His Spirit to transform our moans, groans, and sighs into the profoundest prayers that reach the depths of God's heart. "The Spirit helps us in our weakness. . . . [T]he Spirit himself intercedes for us with sighs too deep for words" (Rom. 8:26).

We need to pray better, because that is the only way we can live better. It is sometimes said that prayer is the breath of the spiritual life. That's partially true. It would be more true to say that it is the breath, food, rest, shelter, and means of begetting in the spiritual life. Prayer, then, is the very life of the soul. And, since the soul is immortal, the prayer that we build up on earth will be more permanent than any buildings, memorials, cathedrals, or skyscrapers we can raise with bricks, steel, glass, or marble.

Prayer is the way we live our relationship with God. *Covenant* is the word Jesus used to describe this relationship. In the ancient world, a covenant was the legal and ritual means of establishing a family bond. Marriage was considered a covenant; so was adoption. Covenant, then, makes us share in the life of the eternal Family of God, the Blessed Trinity.

We often pray so that something will change. We pray for a healing, a promotion, a reconciliation, a deliverance. All of these are changes.

A covenant, indeed, always changes something. It changes a relationship by changing the status of one of the parties. And what is it that changes when we pray? Often, it seems that people pray in order to change God's mind. But God is eternal, perfect, unchanging, and unchangeable. We pray so that God can change *our* minds.

Prayer is the way we live our covenant, and so every prayer changes something. It changes us because it intensifies our relationship with God. If the Spirit can change our moans and groans into prayer, then the Spirit can also change our minds, hearts, and wills through prayer—and He'll do this in a way that cannot happen apart from prayer.

We pray in order to become saints. That's what it means to have an intense relationship with God. Sainthood is the one thing we're here on earth to acquire. It's the only thing we can take away from here.

So learn from the saints who have gone before us. They've prayed the Lord's Prayer and have enjoyed its effects most abundantly. We have the Church's infallible word on that. But which saints should we study? The best place to start is at the beginning, with our very eldest brothers in Christ, the brothers we call our fathers: the Fathers of the Church. I would rather lead you to learn from them than from me.

It's humbling to have my thoughts included within the same covers as theirs. But it will be well worth the humiliation if the end result is that you keep reading—and that you discover the giants upon whose shoulders I stand. Every great boxing match or concert begins with a warm-up act before the main event.

I'd like to draw your attention to three themes that recur in the following pages from the Fathers.

First in importance is the centrality of divine father-hood and our share—our real participation—in Christ's divine sonship.

Next, notice how the Fathers insist that our goal is virtue, and not mere learning. They're speaking, moreover, not just of the virtues that make us more prosperous: honesty, diligence, thrift, patience, and so on. They want us especially to grow in the possession and practice of the theological virtues: faith, hope, and charity. To live these virtues means, quite simply, to live as a child of God.

Finally, learn to appreciate the unity of the Old and New Covenants. Note that all the texts included in this volume are biblical reflections, not merely New Testament reflections. The New Covenant is promised in the old, and the old is fulfilled in the new. Typology is the principle by which we see this most clearly (cf. Catechism, nos. 128-130). Typology shows us that passing from the Old to the New is more than just turning a page from Second Maccabees to Matthew. Typology shows us how Jesus' coming, in the fullness of time, represents the hinge of history—world history and personal history, your life and mine. Typology is not just a literary device, not just an interpretive key to a difficult book. Typology means something intimate for all of us, our movement from servitude to sonship, from time to eternity, from the natural to the supernatural, from earth to heaven . . . from our Creator to our Father.

— PART II —

WISDOM FROM THE FATHERS OF THE CHURCH

SAINT CYPRIAN

Treatise on the Lord's Prayer (selection)

The evangelical precepts, beloved brethren, are nothing else than divine teachings—foundations on which hope is to be built, supports to strengthen faith, nourishments for cheering the heart, rudders for guiding our way, guards for obtaining salvation. While these precepts instruct the docile minds of believers on earth, they lead them to heavenly kingdoms. God, moreover, willed many things to be said and heard by means of His servants, the prophets; but how much greater are those precepts which the Son speaks, which the Word of God, Who was in the prophets, testifies with His own voice. He does not now bid us prepare the way for His coming, but He Himself comes, opening and showing us the way, so that we, who have previously been wandering blindly and without forethought in the darkness of death, might be enlightened by the light of grace and keep the way of life, with the Lord as our Ruler and Guide.

Among His salutary admonitions and divine precepts with which He counsels His People for their salvation, He Himself also revealed a form of praying, and He advised and instructed us about what we should pray for. He Who made us to live also taught us to pray, with that same benignity with which He has condescended to give and confer all other things, in order that while we speak to the

Father in that prayer and supplication which the Son has taught us, we may be more readily heard. Already He had foretold that the hour was coming "when the true worshipers will worship the Father in spirit and in truth" (Jn. 4:23), and He thus fulfilled what He previously promised, so that we who by His sanctification have received the Spirit and truth may also by His teaching worship truly and spiritually. For what can be a more spiritual prayer than that which was given to us by Christ, by Whom also the Holy Spirit was given to us? What praying to the Father can be more truthful than that which was delivered to us by the Son, Who is the Truth, out of His own mouth? To pray in another manner than He taught is not only ignorance, but also sin, since He Himself has established, "You have a fine way of rejecting the commandment of God, in order to keep your tradition" (Mk. 7:9).

Let us, therefore, beloved brethren, pray as God our Teacher has taught us. It is a loving and friendly prayer to beseech God with His own words, for the prayer of Christ to ascend to His ears. Let the Father acknowledge the words of His Son when we make our prayer, and let Him Who dwells within our breast also dwell in our voice. And since we have Him as an Advocate for our sins with the Father, let us, when as sinners we petition on behalf of our sins, put forward the words of our Advocate. Since He says that "if you ask anything of the Father, he will give it to you in my name" (Jn. 16:23), how much more effectually do we obtain what we ask in Christ's name, if we ask for it in His own prayer!

But let our speech and petition when we pray be under discipline, observing quietness and modesty. Let us consider that we are standing in God's sight. We must please the divine eyes both with the habit of body and with the measure of voice. For as it is characteristic of a shameless man to be noisy with his cries, so, on the other hand, it is fitting for the modest man to pray with moderated petitions.

Moreover, in His teaching the Lord has bidden us pray in secret—in hidden and remote places, in our very bedchambers—which is best suited to faith, that we may know that God is present everywhere, hears and sees all, and penetrates even into hidden and secret places in the plenitude of His majesty, as it is written: "Am I a God at hand, says the LORD, and not a God far off? Can a man hide himself in secret places so that I cannot see him? says the LORD. Do I not fill heaven and earth?" (Jer. 23:23-24). And again, "The eyes of the LORD are in every place, keeping watch on the evil and the good" (Prov. 15:3).

When we meet together with the brethren in one place and celebrate divine sacrifices with God's priest, we ought to be mindful of modesty and discipline—not to scatter our prayers indiscriminately, with unsubdued voices, nor to offer to God with tumultuous wordiness a petition that ought to be commended to Him by modesty (for God is the Hearer, not of the voice, but of the heart). Nor need He be reminded clamorously, since He sees men's thoughts, as the Lord proves to us when He says, "Why do you think evil in your hearts?" (Mt. 9:4), and in another place, "And all the churches shall know that I am he who searches mind and heart" (Rev. 2:23).

And in the First Book of Samuel, Hannah, who was a type of the Church, maintains and observes this discipline of prayer, in that she prayed to God not with clamorous petition, but silently and modestly, within the very recesses of her heart. She spoke with hidden prayer, but with manifest faith. She spoke not with her voice, but with her heart, because she knew that in this way God hears; and she effectually obtained what she sought, because she asked for it with belief. Divine Scripture asserts this when it says, "Hannah was speaking in her heart; only her lips moved, and her voice was not heard. . . . and the LORD remembered her" (1 Sam. 1:13, 19). We read also in the Psalms, "[C]ommune with your own hearts on your beds, and be silent" (Ps. 4:4). The Holy Spirit, moreover, suggests these same things by Jeremiah and teaches, "But say in your heart, 'It is thou, O Lord, whom we must worship'" (Bar. 6:6).

And let not the worshiper, beloved brethren, be ignorant of the manner in which the tax collector prayed with the Pharisee in the Temple. Not with eyes lifted up boldly to heaven, nor with hands proudly raised, but beating his breast and testifying to the sins within, he implored the help of the Divine Mercy. And while the Pharisee was pleased with himself, the man who asked in this manner instead deserved to be sanctified, since he placed the hope of salvation not in the confidence of his innocence (because there is none who is innocent), but he confessed his sinfulness as he humbly prayed, and He who pardons the humble heard the petitioner. And these things the Lord records in His Gospel:

> Two men went up into the temple to pray, one a Pharisee and the other a tax collector. The Pharisee stood and

prayed thus with himself, "God, I thank thee that I am not like other men, extortioners, unjust, adulterers, or even like this tax collector. I fast twice a week, I give tithes of all that I get." But the tax collector, standing far off, would not even lift up his eyes to heaven, but beat his breast, saying, "God, be merciful to me a sinner!" I tell you, this man went down to his house justified rather than the other; for every one who exalts himself will be humbled, but he who humbles himself will be exalted (Lk. 18:10-14).

Beloved brethren, when we have understood from the sacred reading in what way we ought to approach prayer, let us know also from the Lord's teaching how we should pray:

Pray then like this:
Our Father who art in heaven,
Hallowed be thy name.
Thy kingdom come,
Thy will be done,
On earth as it is in heaven.
Give us this day our daily bread;
And forgive us our debts,
As we also have forgiven our debtors;
And lead us not into temptation,
But deliver us from evil (Mt. 6:9-13).

Before all things, the Teacher of peace and the Master of unity would not wish prayer to be made individually; He would not wish one who prays to pray for himself alone. For we do not say, "My Father who art in heaven," nor, "Give me this day my daily bread," nor does each one ask that only his own debt should be forgiven him, nor does he request for himself alone that he may not be led into temptation and delivered from evil. Our prayer is public and common; and when we pray, we pray not for one, but for the whole People, because we the whole People are one. The God of peace and the Teacher of concord, Who taught unity, willed that one should thus pray for all, even as He Himself bore us all in one.

The three young men observed this law of prayer when they were shut up in the fiery furnace, speaking together in prayer, and being of one heart in the agreement of the Spirit. The teaching of Sacred Scripture assures us of this, and in telling us how such men as these prayed, it gives an example that we ought to follow in our prayers, in order that we may be like them: "Then the three," it says, "as with one mouth, praised and glorified and blessed God" (Dan. 3:28). They spoke as if from one mouth, although Christ had not yet taught them how to pray. And therefore, as they prayed, their speech was availing and effectual, because the Lord deserved a peaceful, sincere, and spiritual prayer.

We also find that the apostles, with the disciples, prayed in this way after the Lord's Ascension: "All of these," says the Scripture, "with one accord devoted themselves to prayer, together with the women and Mary the mother of Jesus, and with his brethren" (Acts 1:14). They continued with one accord in prayer, declaring both by the urgency and by the agreement of their praying that God, "who maketh men of one manner to dwell in a house" (Ps. 67:7, Douay Rheims Version), only admits into the divine and eternal home those whose prayer is unanimous.

But what matters of deep importance are contained in the Lord's Prayer! So many and such great matters, briefly collected in words, but spiritually abundant in virtue—so that there is absolutely nothing passed over that is not comprehended in these our prayers and petitions, as in a compendium of heavenly doctrine. "Pray then like this: Our Father who art in heaven" (Mt. 6:9). The new man, born again and restored to his God by His grace, says, "Father," in the first place because he has now begun to be a son. He says, "He came to his own home, and his own people received him not. But to all who received him, who believed in his name, he gave power to become children of God" (Jn. 1:11-12).

The man, therefore, who has believed in His name and has become God's son ought from this point to begin both to give thanks and to profess himself God's son by declaring that God is his Father in heaven. He also ought to bear witness, among the very first words of his new birth, that he has renounced an earthly and carnal father, and that he has begun to know as a Father (as well as to have as a Father) only Him Who is in heaven, as it is written: "Levi . . . who said of his father and mother, 'I regard them not'; he disowned his brothers, and ignored his children. For they observed thy word, and kept thy covenant" (Deut. 33:8-9). Also, the Lord in His Gospel has commanded us to "call no man your father on earth, for you have one Father, who is in heaven" (Mt. 23:9). And to the disciple who had made mention of his dead father, He replied, "[L]eave the dead to bury their own dead" (Mt. 8:22); for he had said that his father was dead, while the Father of believers is living.

Nor ought we, beloved brethren, only to observe and understand that we should call Him Father Who is in heaven; but we add to it and say, "Our Father," that is, the Father of those who believe—of those who, being sanctified by Him, and restored by the birth of spiritual grace, have begun to be sons of God. . . .

Nor can a sinful people be a son, but the name of sons is attributed to those to whom remission of sins is granted, and to them immortality is promised anew, in the words of our Lord Himself: "[E]very one who commits sin is a slave to sin. The slave does not continue in the house for ever; the son continues for ever" (Jn. 8:34-35).

But how great is the Lord's indulgence! How great His condescension and abundance of goodness towards us, seeing that He has wished us to pray in the sight of God in such a way as to call God "Father," and to call ourselves sons of God, even as Christ is the Son of God—a name which none of us would dare to venture in prayer, unless He Himself had allowed us thus to pray. We ought then, beloved brethren, to remember and know that when we call God "Father," we ought to act as God's children, so that in the measure in which we find pleasure in considering God as a Father, He might also be able to find pleasure in us.

Let us converse as temples of God, that it may be plain that God dwells in us. Let not our doings be degenerate from the Spirit, so that we who have begun to be heavenly and spiritual may consider and do nothing but spiritual and heavenly things. The Lord God Himself has said, "[T]hose who honor me I will honor, and those who despise me shall be lightly esteemed" (1 Sam. 2:30). The blessed apostle also has laid down in his epistle: "You are not your own; you were bought with a price. So glorify God in your body" (1 Cor. 6:19-20).

After this, we say, "Hallowed be thy name" (Mt. 6:9)—not that we wish for God that He may be hallowed by our prayers, but that we beseech Him that His name may be hallowed in us. But by whom is God sanctified, since He Himself sanctifies? Because He says, "Consecrate yourselves therefore, and be holy; for I am the LORD your God" (Lev. 20:7), we do well to ask and entreat that we who were sanctified in baptism may continue in that which we have begun to be. And we daily pray for this, for we have need of daily sanctification, that we who daily fall away may wash out our sins by continual sanctification. And the apostle declares what the sanctification is which is conferred upon us by the condescension of God: "[N]either the immoral, nor idolaters, nor adulterers, nor homosexuals, nor thieves, nor the greedy, nor drunkards, nor revilers, nor robbers will inherit the kingdom of God. And such were some of you. But you were washed, you were sanctified, you were justified in the name of the Lord Jesus Christ and in the Spirit of our God" (1 Cor. 6:9-11).

He says that we are sanctified in the name of our Lord Jesus Christ and by the Spirit of our God. We pray that this sanctification may abide in us. Because our Lord and Judge warns the man who was healed and revived by Him to sin no more, lest a worse thing happen to him, we make this supplication in our constant prayers—we ask it day and night—that the sanctification and revival that is received from the grace of God may be preserved by His protection.

Then "Thy kingdom come" follows in the prayer (Mt. 6:10). We ask that the Kingdom of God may be manifested to us, even as we also ask that His name may be sanctified in us. For when does God not reign, or when does anything begin with Him, Who both always has been and never ceases to be? We pray that our Kingdom, which has been promised us by God, and which was acquired by the Blood and Passion of Christ, may come, so that we who first are His subjects in the world may hereafter reign with Christ when He reigns, as He Himself promises: "Come, O blessed of my Father, inherit the kingdom prepared for you from the foundation of the world" (Mt. 25:34).

Christ Himself, dearest brethren, may be the Kingdom of God, Whom we day by day desire to come, Whose Advent we crave to be quickly manifested to us. For since He is Himself the Resurrection (for in Him we rise again), so also the Kingdom of God may be understood to be Himself, since in Him we shall reign.

But we do well in seeking the Kingdom of God, that is, the heavenly Kingdom, because there is also an earthly kingdom. He who has already renounced the world is, moreover, greater than its honors and its kingdom. And therefore, he who dedicates himself to God and Christ desires not earthly but heavenly kingdoms. But there is need of continual prayer and supplication, that we may not fall away from the heavenly Kingdom, as the Jews, to whom this promise had first been given, fell away—even as the Lord sets forth: "[M]any will come from east and west and sit at table with Abraham, Isaac, and Jacob in the kingdom of heaven, while the sons of the Kingdom will be thrown into the outer darkness; there men will weep and gnash their teeth" (Mt. 8:11-12).

He shows that the Jews were previously children of the Kingdom, so long as they continued also to be children of God; but after the name of Father ceased to be recognized among them, the Kingdom also ceased. Therefore, we Christians, who in our prayer begin to call God our Father, pray also that God's Kingdom may come to us.[1]

We add, "Thy will be done, [o]n earth as it is in heaven" (Mt. 6:10)—not that God should do what He wills, but that we may be able to do what God wills. For who resists God, that He may not do what He wills? But since we are hindered by the Devil from obeying God's will in all things, in our thoughts and deeds, we pray and ask that God's will may be done in us. And that it may be done in us, we have need of God's good will, that is, of His help and protection, since no one is strong in his own strength, but one is safe only by the grace and mercy of God. And further, the Lord, manifesting the infirmity of the humanity which He bore, says, "My Father, if it be possible, let this cup pass from me" (Mt. 26:39), and affording an example to His disciples that they should do not their own will, but God's, He went on to say, "nevertheless, not as I will, but as thou wilt" (Mt. 26:39). And in another place He says, "I have come down from heaven, not to do my own will, but the will of him who sent me" (Jn. 6:38).

---

[1] Far from evoking anti-Semitism, this passage should lead us to realize that if God did not spare the Chosen People of Israel and their beloved capital (Jerusalem, the holy city), we Gentiles will not be spared the same judgment that befell our eldest brother, Israel (cf. Ex. 4:22).

Now if the Son was obedient to do His Father's will, how much more should the servant be obedient to do his Master's will! In his epistle, John also exhorts and instructs us to do the will of God: "Do not love the world or the things in the world. If any one loves the world, love for the Father is not in him. For all that is in the world, the lust of the flesh and the lust of the eyes and the pride of life, is not of the Father but is of the world. And the world passes away, and the lust of it; but he who does the will of God abides for ever" (1 Jn. 2:15-17). We who desire to abide for ever should do the will of God, Who is everlasting.

Now this is the will of God which Christ both did and taught: humility in conversation; steadfastness in faith; modesty in words; justice in deeds; mercifulness in works; discipline in morals; to be unable to do a wrong, and to be able to bear a wrong when done; to keep peace with the brethren; to love God with all one's heart; to love Him because He is a Father, to fear Him because He is God; to prefer nothing whatever to Christ, because He did not prefer anything to us; to adhere inseparably to His love; and to stand by His Cross bravely and faithfully. When there is any contest on behalf of His name and honor, we ought to show in discourse that constancy with which we confess our faith; in torture, to show that confidence with which we do battle; in death, to show that patience with which we are crowned. All this is to desire to be fellow heirs with Christ, to do the commandment of God, and to fulfill the will of the Father.

Moreover, we ask that the will of God may be done both in heaven and on earth, each of which pertains to the fulfillment of our safety and salvation. For since we possess the body from the earth and the spirit from heaven, we ourselves are earth and heaven; and in both—that is, both in body and in spirit—we pray that God's will may be done. For between the flesh and spirit there is a struggle, and there is a daily strife as they disagree with one another, so that we cannot do those very things that we would. The spirit seeks heavenly and divine things, while the flesh lusts after earthly and temporal things. Therefore, we ask that by the help and assistance of God, agreement may be made between these two natures, so that while the will of God is done both in the spirit and in the flesh, the soul which is newborn of Him may be preserved. This is what the apostle Paul openly and manifestly declares:

> For the desires of the flesh are against the Spirit, and the desires of the Spirit are against the flesh; for these are opposed to each other, to prevent you from doing what you would. But if you are led by the Spirit you are not under the law. Now the works of the flesh are plain: immorality, impurity, licentiousness, idolatry, sorcery, enmity, strife, jealousy, anger, selfishness, dissension, party spirit, envy, drunkenness, carousing, and the like. I warn you, as I warned you before, that those who do such things shall not inherit the kingdom of God. But the fruit of the Spirit is love, joy, peace, patience, kindness, goodness, faithfulness, gentleness, self-control (Gal. 5:17-23).

And therefore, we make it our prayer in daily, and even in continual supplications, that the will of God concerning us should be done both in heaven and on earth; for this is the will of God, that earthly things should give place to heavenly, and that spiritual and divine things should prevail.

And it may be thus understood, beloved brethren, that since the Lord commands and admonishes us to love even our enemies, and to pray even for those who persecute us, we should ask, moreover, for those who are still earthly and have not yet begun to be heavenly, that even in them God's will may be done, which Christ accomplished in preserving and renewing humanity. For since the disciples are not now called by Him "earth," but the salt of the earth, and the apostle designates the first man as being from the dust of the earth, but the second from heaven, we reasonably, who ought to be like God our Father (Who makes His sun to rise upon the good and bad, and sends rain upon the just and the unjust), pray and ask by the admonition of Christ in such a manner as to make our prayer for the salvation of all men. Thus, just "as in heaven"—that is, in us by our faith—the will of God has been done (so that we might be of heaven), so also "on earth"—that is, in those who do not believe—may God's will be done, that they who as yet are earthly may be born of water and of the Spirit and begin to be heavenly.

As the prayer goes forward, we ask, "Give us this day our daily bread" (Mt. 6:11). And this may be understood both spiritually and literally, because either way of understanding it is rich in divine usefulness for our salvation. For Christ is the Bread of life; and this Bread does not belong to all men, but is ours. And as we say, "Our Father," because He is the Father of those who understand and believe, so also we call it "our bread," because Christ is the Bread of those who are in union with His Body. And we ask that this Bread be given to us daily, that we who are in Christ and daily receive the Eucharist for the food of salvation may not, by the interposition of some heinous sin, be prevented from receiving Communion and from partaking of the heavenly Bread and be separated from Christ's Body. He Himself warns, "I am the bread of life. . . . This is the bread which comes down from heaven, that a man may eat of it and not die. . . . [I]f any one eats of this bread, he will live for ever; and the bread which I shall give for the life of the world is my flesh" (Jn. 6:48, 50-51). When, therefore, He says that whoever shall eat of His Bread shall live forever, it is manifest that those who partake of His Body and receive the Eucharist by the right of Communion are living. On the other hand, we must fear and pray lest anyone who, being withheld from Communion, be separated from Christ's Body and remain at a distance from salvation, for He Himself threatens, "[U]nless you eat the flesh of the Son of man and drink his blood, you have no life in you" (Jn. 6:53). And therefore, we ask that our Bread—that is, Christ—may be given to us daily, that we who abide and live in Christ may not depart from His sanctification and Body.

But it may also be understood in this way, that we who have renounced the world and who, in the faith of spiritual grace, have cast away its riches and pomps, should only ask for ourselves food and support, since the Lord instructs us, "[W]hoever of you does not renounce all that he has cannot be my disciple" (Lk. 14:33). But he who has begun to be Christ's disciple, renouncing all things according to the word of his Master, ought to ask for his daily food, and not to extend the desires of his petition over a long period, as the Lord again commands, "Therefore do not be anxious about tomorrow, for tomorrow will be anxious for itself.

Let the day's own trouble be sufficient for the day" (Mt. 6:34). With reason, then, does Christ's disciple ask food for himself for the day, since he is prohibited from thinking of the morrow. It becomes a contradiction and a repugnant thing for us to seek to live long in this world, since we ask that the Kingdom of God should come quickly. So also the blessed apostle admonishes us, giving substance and strength to the steadfastness of our hope and faith: "[F]or we brought nothing into the world, and we cannot take anything out the world; but if we have food and clothing, with these we shall be content. But those who desire to be rich fall into temptation, into a snare, into many sense-less and hurtful desires that plunge men into ruin and destruction. For the love of money is the root of all evils; it is through this craving that some have wandered away from the faith and pierced their hearts with many pangs" (1 Tim. 6:7-10).

He teaches us not only that riches are to be condemned, but also that they are full of peril, and that in them is the root of seductive evils that deceive the blindness of the human mind by a hidden deception. God also rebukes the rich fool who thinks of his earthly wealth and boasts of himself in the abundance of his overflowing harvests: "Fool! This night your soul is required of you; and the things you have prepared, whose will they be?" (Lk. 12:20). The fool who was to die that very night was rejoicing in his stores, and he to whom life already was failing was thinking of the abundance of his food. But on the other hand, the Lord tells us that he who sells all his goods and distributes them for the use of the poor becomes perfect and complete and lays up for himself treasure in heaven. The Lord says that a man is able to follow Him and to imitate the glory of His Passion when he is free from hindrance, his loins are girt, and he is involved in no entanglements of worldly possessions. Such a man, when he has given his possessions to God, is now free. Let us thus prepare ourselves and learn to pray, and know from the character of the prayer what we ought to be.

For daily bread cannot be wanting to the righteous man, since it is written, "The LORD does not let the righteous go hungry" (Prov. 10:3), and again, "I have been young, and now am old; yet I have not seen the righteous forsaken or his children begging bread" (Ps. 37:25). And the Lord moreover promises: "Therefore do not be anxious, saying, 'What shall we eat?' or 'What shall we drink?' or 'What shall we wear?' For the Gentiles seek all these things; and your heavenly Father knows that you need them all. But seek first his kingdom and his righteousness, and all these things shall be yours as well" (Mt. 6:31-33).

To those who seek God's Kingdom and righteousness, He promises that all things shall be added. For since all things are God's, nothing will be lacking to him who possesses God, if God Himself be not lacking to him. Thus a meal was divinely provided for Daniel; when he was shut up by the king's command in the den of lions, and in the midst of wild beasts who were hungry, they spared him, and the man of God was fed. Thus Elijah in his flight was nourished both by ravens ministering to him in his solitude and by birds bringing him food in his persecution. And—detestable cruelty of the malice of man—the wild beasts spare, the birds feed, while men lay snares and rage!

After this, we also entreat pardon for our sins, saying, "And forgive us our debts, [a]s we also have forgiven our debtors" (Mt. 6:12). After the supply of food, pardon of sin is also asked for, that he who is fed by God may live in God, and that not only the present and temporal life may be provided for, but the eternal life also, to which we may come if our sins are forgiven. The Lord calls these sins "debts," as He says in His Gospel, "I forgave you all that debt because you besought me" (Mt. 18:32). And how necessarily, how providently and salutarily, are we admonished that we are sinners, since we are compelled to entreat pardon for our sins, and while pardon is asked for from God, the soul recalls its own consciousness of sin! Lest anyone should flatter himself that he is innocent, and by exalting himself should more deeply perish, all are instructed and taught that each man sins daily, since each is commanded to entreat pardon daily for his sins.

Moreover, John in his epistle warns us, "If we say we have no sin, we deceive ourselves, and the truth is not in us. If we confess our sins, he is faithful and just, and will forgive our sins" (1 Jn. 1:8-9). In his epistle, he has written both that we should entreat pardon for our sins and that we should obtain pardon when we ask. Therefore, he said that the Lord was faithful to forgive sins, keeping the faith of His promise, because He who taught us to pray for our debts and sins has promised that His fatherly mercy and pardon shall follow.

He has clearly added a provision to this promise and has bound us by a certain condition: that we should ask that our debts be forgiven us in such a manner as we ourselves forgive our debtors. We know that what we seek for our sins cannot be obtained unless we ourselves have acted in a similar way to our debtors. Therefore, He says in another place, "[W]ith the judgment you pronounce you will be judged, and the measure you give will be the measure you get" (Mt. 7:2). And the servant who, after having had all his debt forgiven him by his master, would not forgive his fellow servant is cast back into prison; because he would not forgive his fellow servant, he lost the indulgence that had been shown to himself by his lord.

Christ still more urgently sets forth these things in His precepts. "And whenever you stand praying," He says, "forgive, if you have anything against any one; so that your Father also who is in heaven may forgive you your trespasses" (Mk. 11:25). There remains no ground of excuse on the Day of Judgment, when you will be judged according to your own sentence; and whatever you have done, you also will suffer. For God commands us to be peacemakers, and in agreement, and of one mind in His house (cf. Ps. 67:7, Douay Rheims Version). In the same manner, He makes us by a second birth, and He wishes us when newborn to continue, that we who have begun to be sons of God may abide in God's peace, and that, having one Spirit, we should also have one heart and one mind. Thus, God does not receive the sacrifice of a person who is in disagreement, but commands him to go back from the altar and first be reconciled to his brother, so that God also may be appeased by the prayers of a peacemaker. Our peace and brotherly agreement are the greater sacrifice to God—being a People united in one, in the unity of the Father, and of the Son, and of the Holy Spirit.

For even in the sacrifices which Abel and Cain first offered, God looked not at their gifts, but at their hearts; so he who was acceptable in his heart was acceptable in his gift. Abel, peaceable and righteous in sacrificing in innocence to God, taught others also that when they bring their gift to the altar, they should come with the fear of God, with a simple heart, with the law of righteousness, and with the peace of concord. With reason, Abel, who so pleased God by his sacrifice, became subsequently himself a sacrifice to God, so that he who first manifested martyrdom and initiated the Lord's Passion by the glory of his blood had both the Lord's righteousness and His peace.

Finally, such are crowned by the Lord, such will be avenged by the Lord on the Day of Judgment; but the quarrelsome and disunited, and he who has not peace with his brethren, in accordance with what the blessed apostle and the Holy Scripture testify—even if he is slain for the name of Christ—shall not be able to escape the crime of fraternal dissension. It is written, "Any one who hates his brother is a murderer" (1 Jn. 3:15), and no murderer attains the Kingdom of heaven, nor does he live with God. He who would rather be an imitator of Judas than of Christ cannot be with Christ. How great is the sin which cannot even be washed away by a baptism of blood—how heinous the crime which cannot be expiated by martyrdom!

Moreover, the Lord admonishes us to say in prayer, "And lead us not into temptation" (Mt. 6:13). In these words, it is shown that the Adversary can do nothing against us unless God has previously permitted it. All our fear, devotion, and obedience should be turned toward God, since in our temptations to evil nothing is permitted unless power is given from Him. This is proved by divine Scripture, which says, "And Nebuchadnezzar king of Babylon came to the city, while his servants were besieging it" (2 Kings 24:11), and the Lord delivered it into his hand. But power is given to evil against us according to our sins, as it is written, "Who gave up Jacob to the spoiler, and Israel to the robbers? Was it not the LORD, against whom we have sinned, in whose ways they would not walk, and whose law they would not obey?" (Is. 42:24). And again, when Solomon sinned and departed from the Lord's commandments and ways, it is recorded, "And the LORD raised up an adversary against Solomon, Hadad the Edomite" (1 Kings 11:14).

Now power is given against us in two modes: either for punishment when we sin, or for glory when we are tested, as we see was done with Job, as God Himself says: "Behold, all that he has is in your power; only upon himself do not put forth your hand" (Job 1:12). And the Lord in His Gospel, at the time of His Passion, says, "You would have no power over me unless it had been given you from above" (Jn. 19:11). But when we ask that we may not be led into temptation, we are reminded of our infirmity and weakness, lest any should insolently vaunt himself, or proudly and arrogantly assume anything to himself, or take to himself as his own the glory of profession of faith or of suffering, when the Lord Himself teaches humility: "Watch and pray that you may not enter into temptation; the spirit indeed is willing, but the flesh is weak" (Mk. 14:38). When a humble and submissive confession comes first, and all is attributed to God, whatever is sought for suppliantly, with fear and honor of God, is granted by His own loving-kindness.

After all these things, in the conclusion of the prayer, comes a brief clause, which briefly and comprehensively sums up all our petitions and our prayers. For we conclude by saying, "But deliver us from evil" (Mt. 6:13), embracing all adverse things which the Enemy attempts against us in this world. There may be a faithful and sure protection from all this adversity if God delivers us, if He affords His help to us who pray for and implore it. And when we say, "Deliver us from evil," there remains nothing further which ought to be asked. When we have once asked for God's protection against evil and have obtained it, then we stand secure and safe against everything which the Devil and the world work against us. For what fear does a man have in this life, if his guardian in this life is God?

What wonder is it, beloved brethren, if such is the prayer which God taught, since in his teaching He condensed all our prayer into one saving sentence? This had already been foretold by Isaiah the prophet, when, being filled with the Holy Spirit, he spoke of the majesty and loving-kindness of God, "consummating and shortening His word," he says, "in righteousness, because a shortened word will the Lord make in the whole earth" (Saint Cyprian's version of Isaiah 10:22-23). For when the Word of God, our Lord Jesus Christ, came to all, gathered alike the learned and unlearned, and proclaimed to every sex and every age the precepts of salvation, He made a large compendium of His precepts, that the memory of scholars might not be burdened in celestial learning, and that they might quickly learn what was necessary for simple faith. Thus, when He taught what eternal life is, He embraced the sacrament of life in a large and divine brevity, saying, "And this is eternal life, that they know thee the only true God, and Jesus Christ whom thou hast sent" (Jn. 17:3). Also, when He gathered from the Law and the Prophets the first and greatest commandments, He said: "You shall love the Lord your God with all your heart, and with all your soul, and with all your mind. This is the great and first commandment. And a second is like it, You shall love your neighbor as yourself. On these two commandments depend all the law and the prophets" (Mt. 22:37-40). And again: "So whatever you wish that men would do to you, do so to them; for this is the law and the prophets" (Mt. 7:12).

The Lord taught us to pray not only by words, but also by deeds. He prayed and besought frequently and thus showed us, by the testimony of His example, what we ought to do, as it is written, "But he withdrew to the wilderness and prayed" (Lk. 5:16). And again: "In these days he went out into the hills to pray; and all night he continued in prayer to God" (Lk. 6:12). But if He Who was without sin prayed, how much more ought sinners to pray; and if He prayed continually, watching through the whole night in uninterrupted petitions, how much more ought we to watch nightly in constantly repeated prayer!

But the Lord prayed and besought not for Himself— for why should He Who was guiltless pray on His own behalf?—but for our sins, as He Himself declared when He said to Peter, "Simon, Simon, behold, Satan demanded to have you, that he might sift you like wheat, but I have prayed for you that your faith may not fail" (Lk. 22:31-32). And subsequently He beseeches the Father for all, saying, "I do not pray for these only, but also for those who believe in me through their word, that they all may be one; even as thou, Father, art in me, and I in thee, that they also may be in us" (Jn. 17:20). The Lord's loving-kindness, no less than His mercy, is great with regard to our salvation. Not content to redeem us with His Blood, He also prayed for us. This was the desire of His petition: that as the Father and Son are one, so also we should abide in absolute unity, so that from this it may be understood how greatly he who divides unity and peace sins, since this unity even the Lord besought, desiring that His People should thus be saved and live in peace. He knew that discord cannot come into the Kingdom of God.

Moreover, when we stand praying, beloved brethren, we ought to be watchful and earnest with our whole heart, intent on our prayers. Let all carnal and worldly thoughts pass away, and do not let the soul at that time think about anything but the object of its prayer. For this reason, the priest, by way of preface before his prayer, prepares the minds of the brethren by saying, "Lift up your hearts," that so upon the people's response, "We lift them up to the Lord," he may be reminded that he himself ought to think of nothing but the Lord.

Let the breast be closed against the Adversary and be open to God alone; do not let it permit God's Enemy to approach it at the time of prayer. For frequently he steals upon us and penetrates within, and by crafty deceit calls away our prayers from God, that we may have one thing in our heart and another in our voice, when not merely the sound of the voice, but also the soul and mind, ought to be praying to the Lord with a simple intention. What carelessness it is to be distracted and carried away by foolish and profane thoughts when you are praying to the Lord—

as if there were anything which you should be thinking of except that you are speaking with God! How can you ask to be heard by God, when you do not hear yourself? Do you wish that God should remember you when you ask, if you do not remember yourself? This is absolutely to take no precaution against the Enemy; to pray to God in this way is to offend the majesty of God by the carelessness of your prayer. It is to be watchful with your eyes and to be asleep with your heart, while the Christian, even though he is asleep with his eyes, ought to be awake with his heart, as it is written in the person of the Church speaking in the Song of Solomon, "I slept, but my heart was awake" (Song 5:2). Therefore, the apostle anxiously and carefully warns us, "Continue steadfastly in prayer, being watchful in it with thanksgiving" (Col. 4.2)—teaching and showing that those whom God sees to be watchful in their prayer are able to obtain from God what they ask.

Moreover, those who pray should not come to God with fruitless or naked prayers. Petition is ineffectual when a barren entreaty beseeches God. For as every tree that does not bring forth fruit is cut down and cast into the fire, words that do not bear fruit cannot deserve anything from God, because they are fruitful in no result. And thus Holy Scripture instructs us, "Prayer is good when accompanied by fasting, almsgiving, and righteousness" (Tob. 12:8). He Who will give us in the Day of Judgment a reward for our labors and alms is even in this life a merciful hearer of one who comes to Him in prayer associated with good works. Thus, for instance, when Cornelius the centurion prayed, he had a claim to be heard. For he was in the habit of giving many alms to the people and of ever praying to God.

When this man prayed at about the ninth hour, an angel bearing testimony to his labors appeared to him and said, "Your prayers and your alms have ascended as a memorial before God" (Acts 10:4).

Those prayers that the merits of our labors urge upon God quickly ascend to Him. Thus also Raphael the angel was a witness to the constant prayer and the constant good works of Tobit:

> I will not conceal anything from you. I have said, "It is good to guard the secret of a king, but gloriously to reveal the works of God." And so, when you and your daughter-in-law Sarah prayed, I brought a reminder of your prayer before the Holy One; and when you buried the dead, I was likewise present with you. When you did not hesitate to rise and leave your dinner in order to go and lay out the dead, your good deed was not hidden from me, but I was with you. So God sent me to heal you and your daughter-in-law Sarah. I am Raphael, one of the seven holy angels who present the prayers of the saints and enter into the presence of the glory of the Holy One (Tob. 12:11-15).

The Lord also teaches similar things by Isaiah:

> Is not this the fast that I choose: to loose the bonds of wickedness, to undo the thongs of the yoke, to let the oppressed go free, and to break every yoke? Is it not to share your bread with the hungry, and bring the homeless poor into your house; when you see the naked, to cover him, and not to hide yourself from your own flesh? Then shall your light break forth like the dawn, and your healing shall spring up speedily; your righteousness shall go before you, the glory of the LORD shall be your rear

guard. Then you shall call, and the LORD will answer; you shall cry, and he will say, Here I am (Is. 58:6-9).

He promises that He will be near and says that He will hear and protect those who, in hearing what God commands to be done, loosen the knots of unrighteousness from their hearts and give alms among the members of God's Household according to His commands, and thus themselves deserve to be heard by God. The blessed apostle Paul, when aided by his brethren in his necessity, said that good works that are performed are sacrifices to God. "I am filled," he says, "having received of Epaphroditus the gifts you sent, a fragrant offering, a sacrifice acceptable and pleasing to God" (Phil. 4:18). When one has pity on the poor, one lends to God; and he who gives to the least gives to God—he sacrifices spiritually to God a fragrant offering.

And in discharging the duties of prayer, we find that the three young men with Daniel, who were strong in faith and victorious in captivity, observed the third, sixth, and ninth hours, which were a sacrament (as it were) of the Trinity, Which in the last times was to be manifested.[2] For the first hour in its progress to the third manifests the consummated number of the Trinity, and the fourth proceeding to the sixth declares another Trinity; and when from the seventh, the ninth is completed, the perfect Trinity is numbered every three hours. The worshipers of God in time past spiritually decided on these spaces of hours as determined and lawful times for prayer. And

---

[2] The hours of the day were numbered from dawn until dusk. The third hour marked midmorning; the sixth, midday; and the ninth, midafternoon.

subsequently it was manifested that these things were sacraments of old, since in olden times righteous men prayed in this manner. The Holy Spirit, Who fulfilled the grace of the Lord's promise, descended upon the disciples at the third hour. Moreover, at the sixth hour, Peter, going up to the housetop, was instructed both by a sign and by the word of God, which admonished him to receive all men into the grace of salvation, whereas he was previously doubtful about receiving the Gentiles into baptism. And from the sixth hour to the ninth, the Lord, being crucified, washed away our sins by His Blood, and that He might redeem us and bring us to life, He then accomplished His victory by His Passion.

But for us, beloved brethren, in addition to the hours of prayer observed of old, both the times and the sacraments have now increased in number. For we must also pray in the morning, that the Lord's Resurrection may be celebrated by morning prayer. And the Holy Spirit previously revealed this in the Psalms: "[M]y King, and my God, for to thee do I pray. O LORD, in the morning thou dost hear my voice; in the morning I prepare a sacrifice for thee, and watch" (Ps. 5:2-3). And again, the Lord speaks by the mouth of the prophet: "Early in the morning shall they watch for me, saying, 'Let us go, and return unto the Lord our God'" (Saint Cyprian's version of Hosea 6:1). Also, at the setting of the sun and at the decline of day, we must of necessity pray again. Since Christ is the true Sun and the true Day, when we pray and ask that light may return to us again as the worldly sun and worldly day depart, we pray for the Advent of Christ, which shall give us the grace of everlasting light. Moreover, the Holy Spirit in the Psalms manifests that Christ is called the Day: "The stone which the builders rejected has become the head of the corner. This is the LORD's doing; it is marvelous in our eyes. This is the day which the LORD has made; let us rejoice and be glad in it" (Ps. 118:22-24).

The prophet Malachi testifies also that He is called the Sun: "But for you who fear my name the sun of righteousness shall rise, with healing in its wings" (Mal. 4:2). But if in the Holy Scriptures Christ is the true Sun and the true Day, there is no hour when Christians ought not frequently and always worship God, so that we who are in Christ—that is, in the true Sun and the true Day—should be constant throughout the entire day in petitions and should pray. When, by the law of the world, the revolving night, recurring in its alternate changes, takes place, there can be no harm arising from the darkness of night to those who pray, because the children of light have the Day even in the night. For if one has light in his heart, when is one not to have light? Or when does he, whose Sun and Day is Christ, not have the Sun and the Day?

Let us not, then, who are in Christ—that is, always in the light—cease from praying even during night. Thus, the widow Anna, constantly praying and watching, persevered in deserving well from God, as it is written in the Gospel: "She did not depart," it says, "from the temple, worshiping with fasting and prayer night and day" (Lk. 2:37). Let the Gentiles who are not yet enlightened look to this, as well as the Jews, who have remained in darkness because they forsook the light. Beloved brethren, let us reckon rightfully—we who are always in the light of the Lord and who remember and hold fast to what we have begun to be by the grace we have received. Let us believe that we always walk in the light and not be hindered by the darkness which we have escaped. Let there be no failure of prayers in the hours of night, no idle and reckless waste of the occasions of prayer. Newly created and newborn of the Spirit by the mercy of God, let us imitate what we shall one day be. Since in the Kingdom we shall possess Day alone, without intervention of night, let us so watch in the night as if it were the daylight. Since we are to pray and give thanks to God forever, let us also not cease in this life to pray and give thanks.

CHAPTER FIFTEEN

SAINT CYRIL OF JERUSALEM

Mystagogic Catechesis V (selection)

We say the prayer that the Savior delivered to His own disciples. With a pure conscience, we call God our Father and say, "Our Father who art in heaven" (Mt. 6:9). O most surpassing loving-kindness of God! On those who revolted from Him and were in very extreme misery, He has bestowed such a complete forgiveness of evil deeds, and such a great participation of grace, that they could even call Him "Father."

"Our Father who art in heaven" (Mt. 6:9). Those who bear the image of the heavenly (cf. 1 Cor. 15:49), in whom God dwells and walks (cf. Is. 52; Rom. 2:24), are a heaven.

"Hallowed be thy name" (Mt. 6:9). The name of God is in its nature holy, whether we say so or not. Since it is sometimes profaned among sinners (according to the words, "The name of God is blasphemed among the Gentiles because of you" [Rom. 2:24]), we pray that in us God's name may be hallowed—not that it comes to be holy from not being holy, but because it becomes holy in us, when we are made holy and do things worthy of holiness.

"Thy kingdom come" (Mt. 6:10). A pure soul can say with boldness, "Thy kingdom come," for he who has heard Paul saying, "Let not sin therefore reign in your mortal bodies" (Rom. 6:12), and has cleansed himself in deed, thought, and word, will say to God, "Thy kingdom come."

"Thy will be done, [o]n earth as it is in heaven" (Mt. 6:10). God's divine and blessed angels do the will of God, as David said in the psalm, "Bless the LORD, O you his angels, you mighty ones who do his word" (Ps. 103:20). So in effect you mean this by your prayer: "As in the angels Thy will is done, so likewise be it done on earth in me, O Lord."

"Give us this day our substantial bread" (cf. Mt. 6:11). Common bread is not substantial bread, but holy Bread is substantial, that is, intended for the substance of the soul. For this Bread goes not into the belly and is cast out into the sewer (cf. Mt. 15:17), but is distributed into your whole person for the benefit of body and soul. By "this day," he means, "each day," as also Paul said, while it is called today (cf. Heb. 3:15).

"And forgive us our debts, [a]s we also have forgiven our debtors" (Mt. 6:12). We have many sins; we offend both in word and in thought; we do very many things worthy of condemnation; and if we say that we have no sin, we lie, as John says (cf. 1 Jn. 1:8). And we make a covenant with God, entreating Him to forgive us our sins, as we also forgive our neighbors their debts. Considering, then, what we receive and what we attain in return, let us not put off, nor delay, forgiving one another. The offenses committed against us are slight and trivial, and easily settled; but those which we have committed against God are great and require such mercy as only He can offer. Take heed, therefore, lest for the slight and trivial sins against you, you shut out forgiveness from God for your very grievous sins.

"And lead us not into temptation" (Mt. 6:13), O Lord. Does the Lord teach us to pray, that we may not be tempted at all? Why, then, is it said elsewhere, "What doth he know, that hath not been tried?" (Sir. 34:9, Douay Rheims Version); and again, "Count it all joy, my brethren, when you meet various trials" (Jas. 1:2)? But does entering into temptation mean being overwhelmed by the temptation? For temptation is, as it were, like a raging winter stream that is difficult to cross. Those, therefore, who are not overwhelmed in temptations pass through the stream and prove themselves excellent swimmers, not being swept away by them at all; while those who are not excellent swimmers enter into temptations and are overwhelmed. For example, Judas entered into the temptation of the love of money and did not swim through it, but was overwhelmed and was strangled both in body and in spirit. Peter entered into the temptation of the denial; but having entered, he was not overwhelmed by it, but manfully swam through it, and was delivered from the temptation. Listen again, in another place, to a company of saints, who give thanks for deliverance from temptation: "For thou, O God, hast proved us: thou hast tried us by fire, as silver is tried. Thou hast brought us into a net, thou hast laid afflictions on our back: thou hast set men over our heads. We have passed through fire and water, and thou hast brought us out into a refreshment" (Ps. 65:10-12, Douay Rheims Version). You see them speaking boldly, because they have passed through and have not been pierced. But "Thou hast brought us out into a refreshment." Their coming into a refreshment is their being delivered from temptation.

"But deliver us from evil" (Mt. 6:13). If "lead us not into temptation" implied not being tempted at all, He would not have said, "But deliver us from evil." Now "evil" is our Adversary, the Devil, from whom we pray to be delivered.

Then after completing the prayer, you say, "Amen"; by this "Amen," which means "so be it," you set your seal to the petitions of this divinely taught prayer.

SAINT JOHN CHRYSOSTOM

Homily XIX on the Gospel of Saint Matthew (selection)

"Pray then like this," He says: "Our Father who art in heaven" (Mt. 6:9). See how He immediately attracted the attention of the hearer and reminded him of all God's bounty. For to call God "Father" is to acknowledge the remission of sins and the taking away of punishment, as well as righteousness, sanctification, redemption, adoption, inheritance, brotherhood to the Only-begotten, and the gift of the Spirit. For one cannot call God "Father" without having attained to all those blessings. He awakens the spirits of His hearers, therefore, in two ways: He reminds them of the dignity of Him Who is called upon, and He reminds them of the greatness of the benefits they have enjoyed.

But when He says, ". . . in heaven," He says this not to limit God to the heavens, but to withdraw from the earth the one who is in prayer, and to fix him in the high places and in the dwellings above.

He teaches us, moreover, to make our prayer common, on behalf of our brethren also. For He does not say, "My Father who art in heaven," but, "Our Father . . ." He teaches each of us to offer up his supplications for the Body in common and in no way to look to our own good, but everywhere to our neighbor's good. And by this petition, He at once takes away hatred, quells pride, casts out envy, brings in the mother of all good things (charity), exterminates the inequality of human things, and shows how far the equality reaches between the king and the poor man. For in those things that are greatest and most indispensable, all of us are equal. What harm comes to our kindred below, when in what is on high all of us are knit together, and no one has anything more than another— neither the rich more than the poor, nor the master than the servant, neither the ruler than the subject, nor the king than the common soldier, neither the philosopher than the barbarian, nor the skillful than the unlearned? For to all men He has given one nobility, having granted us all alike the privilege of calling Him "Father."

When, therefore, He has reminded us of this nobility, of the gift from above, of our equality with our brethren, and of charity, and when He has removed us from earth and fixed us in heaven, let us see what He commands us to ask after this—even though that saying alone is sufficient to implant instruction in all virtue. For he who has called God "Father," and a common Father, would be justly bound to show forth such a way of life so as not to appear unworthy of this nobility and to exhibit a diligence proportionate to the gift.

"Hallowed be thy name" (Mt. 6:9). It is worthy of him who calls God "Father" to ask nothing before the glory of His Father and to account all things secondary to the work of praising Him. "Hallowed" means glorified. God's own glory is complete and ever continues the same, but He commands him who prays to seek that He may be glorified also by our lives. He had said this very thing before: "Let your light so shine before men, that they may see your good works and give glory to your Father who is in heaven"

(Mt. 5:16). The seraphim, too, give glory: "Holy, holy, holy" (Is. 6:3; Rev. 4:8). "Hallowed," then, means "glorified." In other words, He says, "Grant that we may live so purely, that through us all may glorify You." Living such a life is the result of perfect self-control—to manifest to all a life so blameless that everyone who sees our life may offer to the Lord the praise due to Him for this blamelessness.

"Thy kingdom come" (Mt. 6:10). This, too, is the language of a right-minded child of God, not to be attached to things that are seen, nor to account present things as some great matter, but to hasten to our Father and to long for the things to come. This petition springs from a good conscience and a soul set free from earthly things. Paul himself, for instance, was longing after this every day. Therefore, he also said that "we ourselves who have the first fruits of the Spirit groan inwardly as we wait for adoption as sons, the redemption of our bodies" (Rom. 8:23). For he who has this desire can neither be puffed up by the good things of this life nor abashed by its sorrows. As though dwelling in the very heavens, such a man is freed from all kinds of unreasonable desires.

"Thy will be done, [o]n earth as it is in heaven" (Mt. 6:10). Behold a most excellent train of thought! He commanded us indeed both to long for the things to come and to hasten on that journey to heaven. Until that day, while we abide here, He commands us to be earnest in manifesting the same way of life as those above. For you must long, He says, for heaven, and the things in heaven; however, even before heaven, He has commanded us to make the earth a heaven and do and say all things, even while we are continuing to live on earth, as if we were living in heaven. This, too, should be an object of our prayer to the Lord. For there is nothing to hinder our reaching the perfection of the powers above, simply because we inhabit the earth; but it is possible, even while abiding here, to do everything as if we were already placed on high. What He means, therefore, is this: "As in heaven all things are done without hindrance, and the angels are not partly obedient and partly disobedient, but in all things yield and obey (for He says, 'Mighty in strength, performing His word' [cf. Ps. 103:20]), so grant that we men may not do Your will by halves, but do all things as You will."

Do you see how He has taught us also to be modest, by making it clear that virtue comes not only from our endeavors, but also from the grace from above? And again, He has enjoined each one of us who prays to take upon himself the care of the whole world. For He did not at all say, "Thy will be done in me" or "in us," but everywhere on the earth, so that error may be destroyed, truth may be implanted, all wickedness may be cast out, virtue may be returned, and there be no difference in these respects, henceforth, between heaven and earth. "For if this comes to pass," He says, "there will be no difference between things below and above, separated as they are in nature; the earth will exhibit to us another set of angels."

"Give us this day our daily bread" (Mt. 6:11). What is "daily bread"? Enough bread for one day.

Because He had said, "Thy will be done, [o]n earth as it is in heaven" (Mt. 6:10), and was conversing with men made of flesh, subject to the necessities of nature, and incapable of the same impassibility as the angels possess—and He enjoins the commands to be fulfilled by us also, even as the angels perform them—He also takes into account, in the petition that follows, the infirmity of our nature. Thus, He says, "I require as great perfection of conduct from men as I do from angels, but not freedom from passions—no, for the tyranny of nature, which requires necessary food, permits it not." But note how even in things that are bodily, that which is spiritual abounds. It is neither for riches, nor for delicate living, nor for costly raiment, nor for any other such thing, but for bread only that He has commanded us to make our prayer. And we pray for "daily bread," so as not to "be anxious about tomorrow" (Mt. 6:34). Because of this He added "daily bread," that is, bread for one day.

He is not satisfied even with this expression, but adds another—"Give us this day" (Mt. 6:11)—so that we may not wear ourselves out with anxiety for the following day. For why are you anxious about a future day, when you do not know whether you should see it?

He admonishes us more fully about this matter: "[D]o not be anxious about tomorrow" (Mt. 6:34). He would have us be on every hand unencumbered and winged for flight, have us yield only so much to nature as the compulsion of necessity requires of us.

Then, when it comes to pass that we sin even after the washing of regeneration, even then He shows His love for man to be great. He commands us for the remission of our sins to come to God, Who loves man, and to say, "And forgive us our debts, [as] we also have forgiven our debtors" (Mt. 6:12).

Do you not see surpassing mercy here? After taking away such great evils, and after the unspeakable greatness of His gift, He is willing to forgive men who sin again.

That this prayer belongs to believers is taught both by the laws of the Church and by the beginning of the prayer, for the unbaptized could not call God "Father." If, then, the prayer belongs to believers, and they pray, entreating that sins may be forgiven them, it is clear that not even after the sin is the profit of repentance taken away; indeed, had He not meant to signify this, He would not have made a law that we should so pray. He brings sins to remembrance, bids us ask forgiveness, teaches how we may obtain remission, and so makes the way easy. It is perfectly clear, then, that He introduced this rule of supplication, knowing and signifying that it is possible even after the font of Baptism to wash ourselves from our offenses. By reminding us of our sins, He persuades us to be modest; by the command to forgive others, He sets us free from all vengeful passion; by promising in return for this to pardon us also, He holds out good hope and instructs us to recognize the depth of the unspeakable mercy of God towards man.

But what we should most observe is that in each of the clauses He had mentioned the whole of virtue. In this way, He had included also the forgetfulness of injuries—for "His name be hallowed" implies a perfect way of life, and "His will be done" declares the same thing again, and to be able to call God "Father" is the profession of a blameless life. In all these things is included the duty of remitting our anger against those who have transgressed. Still, He was not satisfied with only these petitions, but meaning to signify how earnest He is in the matter, He sets down this admonition in particular, and after the prayer, He mentions no other commandment than this: "For if you forgive men their trespasses, your heavenly Father also will forgive you" (Mt. 6:14).

Thus, forgiveness begins with us, and we ourselves have control over the judgment that is to be passed upon us. In order that no one, even the foolish, might have any complaint to make, either great or small, when brought to judgment, He causes the sentences to depend on you who are to give an account. "[I]f you do not forgive men their trespasses, neither will your Father forgive your trespasses" (Mt. 6:15). And if you forgive your fellow servant, you will obtain the same favor from Me—though indeed the one be not equal to the other. For you forgive in your need, but God has need of nothing; you forgive your fellow slave, God forgives His slave; you are liable for unnumbered charges, God is without sin. Thus, He shows forth His loving-kindness towards man.

He might indeed, even without this, forgive you all your offenses. But He wills you also to receive a benefit, for He affords you on all sides innumerable occasions of gentleness and love to man, in order to cast out what is brutish in you, quench wrath, and in all ways cement you to Him.

For what can you say—that you have wrongfully endured some ill from your neighbor? These only are trespasses; if an act be done with justice, the act is not a trespass. But you, too, are drawing near to receive forgiveness for such things, and for much greater things. Even before the forgiveness, you have received no small gift; you have been taught that you have a human soul and have been trained to all gentleness. A great reward is hereby also laid up for you, in that you are called to account for none of your offenses.

What sort of punishment, then, do we not deserve, when after having received the privilege, we betray our salvation? And how shall we claim to be heard in the rest of our petitions, if we will not in those petitions which depend on us spare ourselves?

"And lead us not into temptation, But deliver us from [the] evil [one]. For thine is the kingdom and the power and the glory, for ever. Amen" (Mt. 6:13).[1]

Here, He teaches us plainly that we are vile, He quells our pride, and He instructs us to seek to avoid all conflicts instead of rushing into them. Thus, our victory will be more glorious, and the Devil's overthrow will be more derided. I mean that when we are dragged forth, we must stand nobly; when we are not summoned, we should be quiet and wait for the time of conflict, that we may show both freedom from vainglory and nobleness of spirit.

And He here calls the Devil "the evil one" and commands us to wage against him a war that knows no truce. He also implies that the Devil is not evil by nature. For wickedness is not of those things that are from nature, but of those things that are added by our own choice. And he is called "evil" preeminently by reason of the excess of his wickedness and because he, in no matter injured by us, wages implacable war against us. Therefore, He did not say, "Deliver us from the evil ones," but He said, "Deliver us from the evil one," instructing us in no case to entertain hatred for our neighbors for whatever wrongs we may suffer at their hands, but to transfer our enmity

---

[1] Alternative reading in footnote *n* of RSVCE.

from these neighbors to the Devil, since he himself is the cause of all our wrongs.

Having then made us prepared for conflict by recalling to our minds the Enemy, and having cut away from us all our negligence, He again encourages us and raises our spirits by bringing to our remembrance the King under Whom we are arrayed and by describing Him as more powerful than all. "For thine," He says, "is the kingdom and the power and the glory" (Mt. 6:13).[2]

Does it not then follow that if the Kingdom be His, we should fear no one, since none can withstand Him and divide the empire with Him? For when He says, "[T]hine is the kingdom," He sets before us the one who is warring against us as one brought into subjection, God for a while permitting him to oppose us. For in truth he, too, is among God's servants, though of the degraded class, and those guilty of offense; and he would not dare attack any of his fellow servants, if he had not first received permission from above. And why do I say "his fellow servants"? Not even against swine did he venture any outrage, until He Himself allowed him (cf. Mt. 8:28-32; Mk. 5:1-13; Lk. 8:26-33); nor against flocks, nor herds, until he had received permission from above.

"And the power," He says. Therefore, manifold as your weakness may be, you may rightly be confident, since you have Someone to reign over you Who is able fully to accomplish all—and easily—even by you.

"And the glory, for ever. Amen." Thus, He not only frees you from the dangers that are approaching you,

---

[2] Alternative reading in footnote *n* of RSVCE.

but also can make you glorious and illustrious. For as His power is great, so also is His glory unspeakable, and His power and glory are all boundless and without end. Do you see how He has by every means anointed His Champion and has appointed Him to be fully worthy of confidence?

Of all the things He loathes, He hates malice most, and He most of all accepts the virtue that is opposed to that vice. Therefore, after the Lord's Prayer, He again recalls this same point of goodness, both by setting a punishment and by appointing a reward, and so urges the hearer to obey this command.

"For if you forgive men their trespasses," He says, "your heavenly Father also will forgive you; but if you do not forgive men their trespasses, neither will your Father forgive your trespasses" (Mt. 6:14-15).

. . . . Not only by grace, but also by works, ought we to become His children. And nothing makes us so like God as being ready to forgive the wicked and wrongdoers, even as indeed He had taught before when He spoke of His Father, Who "makes his sun rise on the evil and on the good" (Mt. 5:45).

SAINT AUGUSTINE

Our Lord's Sermon on the Mount (selection)

But now we have to consider what we are taught to pray for by Him through Whom we both learn what we are to pray for and obtain what we pray for. "Pray then like this," He says:

> Our Father who art in heaven,
> Hallowed be thy name.
> Thy kingdom come,
> Thy will be done,
> On earth as it is in heaven.
> Give us this day our daily bread;
> And forgive us our debts,
> As we also have forgiven our debtors;
> And lead us not into temptation,
> But deliver us from evil (Mt. 6:9-13).

In all prayer, we have to gain the goodwill of Him to Whom we pray; next, we say what we pray for. Goodwill is usually gained when we offer praise to Him to Whom the prayer is directed, and this praise is usually put at the beginning of the prayer. And in this particular, our Lord has commanded us to say nothing else but "Our Father who art in heaven" (Mt. 6:9). For many things are said in praise of God, which, being scattered variously and widely over all the Holy Scriptures, everyone will be able to consider when reading them; yet nowhere is there found a precept for the people of Israel that they should say, "Our Father," or that they should pray to God as a Father. For He was revealed to them as Lord, since they were yet servants, that is, still living according to the flesh.

I say they were servants inasmuch as they received the commands of the Law, which they were ordered to observe. For the prophets often show that this same Lord of ours might have been their Father also, if they had not strayed from His commandments. For instance, we have the statement, "Sons I have reared and brought up, but they have rebelled against me" (Is. 1:2); and, "I say, 'You are gods, sons of the Most High, all of you'" (Ps. 82:6); and, "If then I am a father, where is my honor? And if I am a master, where is my fear?" (Mal. 1:6). In these and very many other statements, the Jews are accused of showing by their sin that they did not wish to become sons. Those things are said in prophecy of a future Christian People, that they would have God as a Father, according to that Gospel statement, "to all who received him . . . he gave power to become children of God" (Jn. 1:12). Again, the apostle Paul says, "[T]he heir, as long as he is a child, is no better than a slave" (Gal. 4:1), and mentions that we have received the Spirit of adoption, "crying, 'Abba! Father!'" (Gal. 4:6).

Because our call to an eternal inheritance—that we might be fellow heirs with Christ and attain to the adoption of sons—is not something we deserve, but is from God's grace, we put this very same grace in the beginning of our prayer when we say, "Our Father." By that appellation, both love (what ought to be dearer to sons than a father?) and a suppliant disposition are stirred up, as is a certain presumption of obtaining what we are about to ask.

Indeed, before we ask anything, we have received the great gift of being allowed to call God our Father. What would He not now give to sons when they ask, when He has already granted this very thing, namely, that they might be sons?

What great solicitude takes hold of the mind, that he who says, "Our Father," should not prove unworthy of so great a Father! For if any plebeian should be permitted to call a senator of more advanced age "father," without a doubt he would tremble and would not readily venture to do it; he would reflect on the humbleness of his origin, the scantiness of his resources, and the worthlessness of his plebeian person. How much more, therefore, ought we to tremble to call God "Father," if there is so great a stain and so much baseness in our character that God might much more justly drive forth these from contact with Himself than a senator might drive forth the poverty of any beggar! Indeed, the senator despises the beggar's poverty, to which even he himself may be reduced by the vicissitude of human affairs, but God never falls into baseness of character. And thanks be to the mercy of Him Who requires this of us, that He should be our Father—a relationship which can be brought about by no expenditure of ours, but solely by God's goodwill. Here also there is an admonition to the rich and to those of noble birth, so far as this world is concerned, that when they have become Christians they should not comport themselves proudly towards the poor and the lowly born, since together with them they call God "our Father"—an expression which they cannot truly and piously use, unless they recognize that they themselves are brethren.

Let the new People, therefore, who are called to an eternal inheritance, use the word of the New Testament, and say, "Our Father who art in heaven," that is, in the holy and the just. For God is not contained in space. The heavens are indeed the higher material bodies of the world, but yet material, and therefore cannot exist except in some definite place; but if God's place is believed to be in the heavens, as meaning the higher parts of the world, the birds are of greater value than we, for their life is nearer to God. But it is not written, "The LORD is near to tall men, or to those who dwell on mountains"; but it is written, "The LORD is near to the brokenhearted" (Ps. 34:18), which refers rather to humility. But as a sinner is called dust, when it is said to him, "[Y]ou are dust, and to dust you shall return" (Gen. 3:19), so, on the other hand, a righteous man may be called "heaven," for it is said to the righteous, "For God's temple is holy, and that temple you are" (1 Cor. 3:17). Therefore, if God dwells in His temple, and the saints are His temple, the expression "who art in heaven" is rightly used in the sense of "who art in the saints." And most suitable is such a comparison, so that spiritually there may be seen to be as great a difference between the righteous and sinners as there is materially between heaven and earth.

In order to show this, we turn to the east, whence the heaven rises, when we stand at prayer. It is not as if God also were dwelling there, in the sense that He Who is everywhere present (not as occupying space, but by the power of His majesty) had forsaken the other parts of the world. But we turn to the east in order that our minds may be admonished to turn to a more excellent nature, that is, to God, when our own bodies, which are earthly, are turned to a more excellent body, that is, to a heavenly one.[1]

It is also suitable for the different stages of religion and expedient in the highest degree that in the minds of all, both small and great, there should be cherished worthy conceptions of God. And therefore, as regards those who as yet are taken up with the beauties that are seen and cannot think of anything incorporeal—inasmuch as they must necessarily prefer heaven to earth—their opinion is more tolerable, if they believe God, Whom as yet they think of after a corporeal fashion, to be in heaven rather than upon earth. Thus, when at any future time they have learned that the dignity of the soul exceeds even that of a celestial body, they may seek Him in the soul rather than in a celestial body. When they have learned as well how great a distance there is between the souls of sinners and of the righteous, just as they did not venture when as yet they were wise only after a carnal fashion to place Him on earth, but in heaven, so afterwards with better faith or intelligence they may seek Him again in the souls of the righteous rather than in those of sinners. Hence, when it is said, "Our Father who art in heaven," it is rightly understood to mean in the hearts of the righteous, as it were in His holy temple. At the same time, he who prays wishes

---

[1] According to Saint Basil the Great (*On the Holy Spirit*, no. 66), Christians have prayed facing the east ever since the time of the apostles. See also Joseph Cardinal Ratzinger, *The Spirit of the Liturgy*, trans. John Saward (San Francisco: Ignatius Press, 2000), 74-84.

Him Whom he invokes to dwell in himself also; when he strives after this, he practices righteousness—a kind of service by which God is attracted to dwell in the soul.

Let us see now what things are to be prayed for. For it has been stated to Whom one prays, and where He dwells.

The first thing prayed for is mentioned in the petition "Hallowed be thy name" (Mt. 6:9). And this is prayed for, not as if the name of God were not holy already, but that it may be held holy by men—that is, that God may so become known to them that they shall reckon nothing more holy, and that there be nothing they are more afraid of offending. Because it is said, "In Judah God is known, his name is great in Israel" (Ps. 76:1), we are not to understand the statement as if God were less in one place, greater in another; but His name is great in that place where He is named according to the greatness of His majesty. And so His name is said to be holy in that place where He is named with veneration and the fear of offending Him. And this is what is now going on as the Gospel, by becoming known everywhere throughout the different nations, commends the name of the one God by means of the ministry of His Son.

In the next place there follows, "Thy kingdom come" (Mt. 6:10). The Lord Himself teaches in the Gospel that the Day of Judgment will take place at the very time when the Gospel will have been preached among all nations (cf. Mt. 24:14)—an action that belongs to the hallowing of God's name. For here also the expression "Thy kingdom come" is not used in such a way as if God were not now reigning. But someone perhaps might say the expression "come" meant "come upon earth"—as if, indeed, He were not even now really reigning upon earth, and had not always reigned upon it from the foundation of the world. "Come," therefore, is to be understood in the sense of "be manifested to men." For in the same way that a light which is present is absent to the blind and to those who shut their eyes, so the Kingdom of God, though it never departs from the earth, is yet absent to those who are ignorant of it. But no one will be allowed to be ignorant of the Kingdom of God when His Only-begotten comes from heaven, not only in a way to be apprehended by the understanding, but also visibly in the Person of the Divine Man, in order to judge the living and the dead. And after that judgment, when the process of distinguishing and separating the righteous from the unrighteous has taken place, God will so dwell in the righteous that there will be no need for anyone to be taught by man, but all will be, as it is written, "taught by the LORD" (Is. 54:13; cf. Jn. 6:45). Then will the blessed life in all its parts be perfected in the saints unto eternity, just as now the most holy and blessed heavenly angels are wise and blessed, since God alone is their Light. The Lord has promised this also to His own: "For in the resurrection," He says, "they . . . are like angels in heaven" (Mt. 22:30).

And therefore, after that petition when we say, "Thy kingdom come," there follows, "Thy will be done, [o]n earth as it is in heaven" (Mt. 6:10). In other words, just as Your will is in the angels who are in heaven, so that they wholly cleave to You and thoroughly enjoy You—no error beclouding their wisdom, no misery hindering their blessedness—so let it be done in Your saints who are on earth and made from the earth, so far as the body is concerned, and who, although it is into a heavenly habitation and exchange, are yet to be taken from the earth. To this there is a reference also in that doxology of the angels, "Glory to God in the highest, and on earth peace among men with whom he is pleased!" (Lk. 2:14). When our goodwill, which follows Him Who calls, has gone before, the will of God is perfected in us as it is in the heavenly angels. Thus, no antagonism stands in the way of our blessedness, and this is peace.

"Thy will be done" is also rightly understood in the sense of "let obedience be rendered to Thy precepts," as in heaven, so on earth, that is, as by the angels, so by men. For the Lord Himself says that the will of God is done when His precepts are obeyed: "My food is to do the will of him who sent me" (Jn. 4:34), and "I have come down from heaven, not to do my own will, but the will of him who sent me" (Jn. 6:38), and "Here are my mother and my brethren! For whoever does the will of my Father in heaven is my brother, and sister, and mother" (Mt. 12:49-50). Therefore, the will of God is accomplished in those who do the will of God, not because they cause God to will, but because they do what He wills, that is, they do according to His will.

There is also that other interpretation of "Thy will be done, [o]n earth as it is in heaven": as in the holy and just, so also in sinners. And this, besides, may be understood in two ways. First, we should pray even for our enemies (for what else are they to be called, since the Christian and Catholic name still spreads in spite of them?), so that it is said, "Thy will be done, [o]n earth as it is in heaven"—as if the meaning were "as the righteous do Thy will, in like manner let sinners also do it, so that they may be converted to You," or "let Thy will be done, on earth as it is in heaven, so that everyone may get his own," which will take place at the Last Judgment, the righteous being requited with a reward, sinners with condemnation—when the sheep shall be separated from the goats (cf. Mt. 25:33, 46).

An additional interpretation is not absurd—indeed, it is thoroughly in accord with both our faith and our hope—that we are to take heaven and earth in the sense of spirit and flesh. And since the apostle says, "I of myself serve the law of God with my mind, but with my flesh I serve the law of sin" (Rom. 7:25), we see that the will of God is done in the mind, that is, in the spirit. But when death shall have been swallowed up in victory and this mortal body shall have put on immortality, which will happen at the resurrection of the flesh and at that change which is promised to the righteous (according to the prediction of the same apostle [cf. 1 Cor. 15:42, 45]), then let the will of God be done on earth, as it is in heaven. In other words, let it follow in such a way that as the spirit does not resist God, but follows and does His will, so the body also may not resist the spirit or soul, which at present is harassed by the weakness of the body and is prone to fleshly habit.

This will be an element of the perfect peace in the life eternal: that not only shall the will be present with us, but also the performance of what is good. "I can will what is right," He says, "but I cannot do it" (Rom. 7:18), for not yet on earth as in heaven (that is, not yet in the flesh as in the spirit) is the will of God done. Even in our misery, the will of God is done, when we suffer those things through the flesh that we deserve in virtue of our mortality and which our nature has deserved because of its sin. But we are to pray that the will of God may be done on earth as in heaven, that as with the heart we delight in the law after the inward man (cf. Rom. 7:22), so also, when the change in our body has taken place, no part of us may, on account of earthly griefs or pleasures, stand opposed to this, our delight.

Nor is still another view inconsistent with truth: that we are to understand the words "Thy will be done, [o]n earth as it is in heaven" as "in our Lord Jesus Christ Himself, so also in the Church"—as if one were to say, "as in the Man Who fulfilled the will of the Father, so also in the woman who is betrothed to Him." Heaven and earth are suitably understood as if they were man and wife, since the earth is fruitful from the heaven fertilizing it.

The fourth petition is "Give us this day our daily bread" (Mt. 6:11). "Daily bread" may mean all those things that meet the wants of this life, in reference to which He teaches, "[D]o not be anxious about tomorrow" (Mt. 6:34)—so that on this account there is added, "Give us this day." It may also mean the Sacrament of the Body of Christ, which we daily receive, or it could mean spiritual food, of which the same Lord says, "Do not labor for the food which perishes" (Jn. 6:27), and, "I am the bread which came down from heaven" (Jn. 6:41).

But which of these three views is the more probable is a question for consideration. Perhaps someone may wonder why we should pray that we may obtain the things that are necessary for this life—for instance, food and clothing—when the Lord Himself says, "[D]o not be anxious about your life, what you shall eat or what you shall drink, nor about your body, what you shall put on" (Mt. 6:25). Can anyone not be anxious for a thing which he prays that he may obtain? Prayer is to be offered with such great earnestness of mind that all that has been said about shutting our closets applies to prayers (cf. Mt. 6:6), as does the command, "But seek first his kingdom and his righteousness, and all these things shall be yours as well" (Mt. 6:33). Certainly He does not say, "Seek first the Kingdom of God, and then seek those other things"; but "all these things," He says, "shall be yours as well," that is to say, even though you are not seeking them. But I do not know whether this can be found out—how one is rightly said not to seek what he most earnestly pleads with God to receive. . . .

It remains, therefore, that we should understand the daily bread as spiritual, divine precepts, which we ought daily to meditate upon and labor after. With respect to these, the Lord says, "Do not labor for the food which perishes, but for the food which endures to eternal life" (Jn. 6:27). That food, moreover, is called daily food at present, so long as this temporal life is measured by means of days that depart and return. So long as the desire of the soul is directed by turns, now to what is higher, now to what is lower, now to spiritual things, now to carnal—as is the case with him who at one time is nourished with food, and at another time suffers hunger—bread is necessary daily in order that the hungry man may be restored, and in order that he who is falling down may be raised up. As our body in this life, before that great change, is replenished with food because it feels loss, so may the soul also be reinvigorated by the food of the precepts, since by means of temporal desires it sustains a loss, as it were, in its striving after God.

Moreover, it is said, "Give us this day," as long as it is called today, that is, in this temporal life. For we shall be so abundantly provided with spiritual food after this life, in eternity, that it will not then be called daily bread. There, the flight of time, which causes days to succeed days (whence it may be called "today"), will not exist. But as it is said, "O that today you would hearken to his voice!" (Ps. 95:7), which the apostle interprets in the Epistle to the Hebrews, "as long as it is called 'today'" (Heb. 3:13), so here also the expression "Give us this day" is to be understood. But if anyone wishes to understand the sentence before us also as meaning food necessary for the body, or of the Sacrament of the Lord's Body, we must take all three meanings conjointly. We are to ask for all three at once as daily bread: the bread necessary for the body, the visible hallowed Bread, and the invisible bread of the word of God.

The fifth petition follows: "And forgive us our debts, [a]s we also have forgiven our debtors" (Mt. 6:12). It is manifest that by "debts," sins are meant, since the Lord Himself makes the statement, "[Y]ou will never get out till you have paid the last penny" (Mt. 5:26), and He called those men "debtors" who were reported to Him as having been killed: those on whom the tower fell, or those whose blood Herod had mingled with the sacrifice. He said that men supposed they died because they were sinners—debtors above measure—and added, "I tell you, No; but unless you repent you will all likewise perish" (Lk. 13:3).

Here, therefore, "debts" is not a money claim that one is urged to forgive, but whatever sins another may have committed against him. For we are enjoined to forgive a money claim by another precept that has been given earlier:

"[I]f any one would sue you and take your coat, let him have your cloak as well" (Mt. 5:40). Nor is it necessary to forgive a debt to every money debtor, but only to him who is unwilling to pay, to such an extent that he wishes even to go to court. "[T]he Lord's servant," as says the apostle, "must not be quarrelsome" (2 Tim. 2:24). Therefore, to him who shall be unwilling, either spontaneously or when requested, to pay the money which he owes, it is to be forgiven. His unwillingness to pay will arise from one of two causes: either that he does not have it or that he is avaricious and covetous of the property of another. Both of these belong to a state of poverty, for the former is poverty of substance, the latter poverty of disposition. Whoever, therefore, forgives such a man's debts forgives one who is poor and performs a Christian work, while the rule remains in force that he should be prepared in his mind to lose what is owed to him. If he has made every attempt, quietly and gently, to have the debt paid back to him, not so much aiming at a money profit as attempting to bring the man round to what is right—without a doubt it is hurtful to him to have the means of paying, and yet not to pay—not only will he not sin, but he will even do a very great service in trying to prevent that other man who is wishing to make gain of another's money from making shipwreck of the faith (and this is so much more serious a thing that there is no comparison).

And hence it is understood that in this fifth petition also when we say, "Forgive us our debts," the words are spoken not indeed in reference to money, but in reference to all the ways in which anyone sins against us, and by consequence in reference to money also. For the man who refuses to pay you the money which he owes, when he has the means of doing so, sins against you. And if you do not forgive this sin, you will not be able to say, "Forgive us, as we also forgive"; but if you pardon it, you see how he who is enjoined to offer such a prayer is admonished also to forgive a monetary debt.

This petition may indeed be construed in another way. When we say, "Forgive us our debts, as we also have forgiven," then we are convicted of having acted contrary to this rule only if we do not forgive those who ask pardon, because we also wish to be forgiven by our most gracious Father when we ask His pardon. But, on the other hand, by that precept whereby we are enjoined to pray for our enemies, it is not for those who ask pardon that we are enjoined to pray, for those who are already in such a state of mind are no longer enemies. It is impossible, however, that one could truthfully say that he prays for one whom he has not pardoned. And therefore we must confess that all sins committed against us are to be forgiven, if we wish those sins which we commit against our Father to be forgiven by Him.

The sixth petition is "And bring us not into temptation" (cf. Mt. 6:13). Some manuscripts have the word "lead," which is, I judge, equivalent in meaning, for both translations have arisen from the one Greek word that is used. But many who pray express themselves thus: "Allow us not to be led into temptation," explaining in what sense the word "lead" is used. For God does not Himself lead, but allows that man whom He has deprived of His assistance to be led into temptation, in accordance with a most hidden arrangement, and with what he deserves. Often, for manifest reasons, He also judges him worthy of being so deprived and allowed to be led into temptation.

But it is one thing to be led into temptation, another to be tempted. For without temptation, no one can be proved—whether to himself, as it is written, "He that is inexperienced knows few things" (Sir. 34:10)—or to another, as the apostle says, "[A]nd though my condition was a trial to you, you did not scorn or despise me" (Gal. 4:14). From this circumstance, Saint Paul learned that they were steadfast; they were not turned aside from charity by those tribulations which had happened to the apostle according to the flesh. For even before all temptations, we are known to God, Who knows all things before they happen.

When, therefore, it is said, "[T]he LORD your God is testing you, to know whether you love the LORD your God with all your heart and with all your soul" (Deut. 13:3), the words "to know" are employed for what is the real state of the case, that He may make you know—just as we speak of a joyful day, because it makes us joyful; of a sluggish frost, because it makes us sluggish; and of innumerable things of the same sort, which are found in ordinary speech, in the discourse of learned men, or in the Holy Scriptures. And the heretics who are opposed to the Old Testament, not understanding this, think that the brand of ignorance, as it were, is to be placed upon Him of Whom it is said, "[T]he LORD your God is testing you"— as if in the Gospel it were not written of the Lord, "This he said to test him, for he himself knew what he would do" (Jn. 6:6). For if He knew the heart of him whom He was tempting, what is it that He wished to see by tempting him? But in reality, the temptation was allowed in order that he who was tempted might become known to himself and that he might condemn his own despair on the multitudes being filled with the Lord's bread, while he had thought they did not have enough to eat.

Here, therefore, the prayer is not that we should not be tempted, but that we should not be brought into temptation, as if, were it necessary that anyone should be examined by fire, he should not pray that he should not be touched by the fire, but that he should not be consumed. For "[t]he kiln tests the potter's vessels; so the test of a man is in his reasoning" (Sir. 27:5). Joseph, therefore, was tempted with the allurement of debauchery, but he was not brought into temptation (cf. Gen. 39:7-12). Susanna was tempted, but she was not led or brought into temptation (cf. Dan. 13:19-23), and so also many others of both sexes. But Job was tempted most of all. In regard to his admirable steadfastness in the Lord his God, those heretical enemies of the Old Testament, when they wish to mock it with sacrilegious mouth, brandish one passage above other weapons: Satan begged that Job should be tempted (cf. Job 1:11). Then these heretics put the question to unskillful men—who are by no means able to understand such things—how Satan could speak with God. These heretics do not understand (for they cannot, inasmuch as they are blinded by superstition and controversy) that God does not occupy space by the mass of His bodiliness. God does not exist in one place, and not in another, or at least have one part here, and another elsewhere, but He is everywhere present in His majesty, not divided by parts, but everywhere complete.

But if they take a fleshly view of what is said ("Heaven is my throne and the earth is my footstool" [Is. 66:1])—to which passage our Lord also bears testimony, when He says, "Do not swear at all, either by heaven, for it is the throne of God, or by the earth, for it is his footstool" (Mt. 5:34-35)—why wonder if the Devil, being placed on earth, stood before the feet of God and spoke something in His presence? When will they be able to understand that there is no soul, however wicked, in whose conscience God does not speak, as long as they can yet reason in any way? For who but God has written the law of nature in the hearts of men? The apostle says of that law: "When Gentiles who have not the law do by nature what the law requires, they are a law to themselves, even though they do not have the law. They show that what the law requires is written on their hearts, while their conscience also bears witness and their conflicting thoughts accuse or perhaps excuse them on that day when, according to my gospel, God judges the secrets of men by Christ Jesus" (Rom. 2:14-16).

And therefore, as in the case of every rational soul that thinks and reasons, even though blinded by passion, we attribute whatever in its reasoning is true, not to itself, but to the very light of truth by which, however faintly, it is illuminated according to its capacity so as to perceive some measure of truth by its reasoning. Why wonder, then, if the depraved spirit of the Devil, perverted though it be by lust, should be represented as having heard from the voice of God Himself (from the voice of the very Truth) whatever true thought it has entertained about a righteous man whom it was proposing to tempt? But whatever is false is to be attributed to that lust from which he has received the name of Devil.

It is also the case that God, as being Lord and Governor of all and Disposer according to the merits of every deed, has often spoken by means of a corporeal and visible creature, whether to good or bad, as, for instance, by means of angels, who appeared also under the aspect of men, and by means of the prophets, saying, "Thus says the Lord." Why wonder, then, if, though not in mere thought, at least by means of some creature fitted for such a work, God is said to have spoken with the Devil?

And let them not imagine it unworthy of God's dignity (and, as it were, of His righteousness) that He spoke with Satan, for He spoke with an angelic spirit, although one foolish and lustful, just as if He were speaking with a foolish and lustful human spirit. Or let such parties themselves tell us how He spoke with that rich man whose most foolish covetousness He wished to censure, saying, "Fool! This night your soul is required of you; and the things you have prepared, whose will they be?" (Lk. 12:20). Certainly, the Lord Himself says so in the Gospel, to which those heretics, whether or not they wish to do so, bend their necks. But if they are puzzled that Satan asks from God that a righteous man should be tempted, I do not explain how it happened, but I compel them to explain why it is said in the Gospel by the Lord Himself to the disciples, "[B]ehold, Satan demanded to have you, that he might sift you like wheat" (Lk. 22:31), and why He says to Peter, "[B]ut I have prayed for you that your faith may not fail" (Lk. 22:32). And when they explain this to me, they explain to themselves at the same time what they question me about. But if they should not be able to explain this, let them not dare with rashness to blame in any book what they read in the Gospel without offense.

Temptations, therefore, take place by means of Satan—not by his power, but by the Lord's permission—either for the purpose of punishing men for their sins, or of proving and exercising them in accordance with the Lord's compassion. And there is a very great difference in the nature of the temptations into which each one may fall. For Judas, who sold his Lord, did not fall into a temptation of the same nature as Peter fell into when, under the influence of terror, he denied his Lord. There are also temptations common to man, I believe, when everyone, though well disposed, yet yielding to human frailty, falls into error in some plan or is irritated against a brother a little more than Christian calmness demands in the earnest endeavor to bring him round to what is right. Concerning these temptations, the apostle says, "No temptation has overtaken you that is not common to man," while he says at the same time, "God is faithful, and he will not let you be tempted beyond your strength, but with the temptation will also provide the way of escape, that you may be able to endure it" (1 Cor. 10:13). In that sentence, he makes it sufficiently evident that we are not to pray that we may not be tempted, but that we may not be led into temptation. For we are led into temptation if such temptations have happened to us that we are not able to bear. But when dangerous temptations, into which it is ruinous for us to be brought and led, arise either from prosperous or adverse temporal circumstances, no one is broken down by the irksomeness of adversity, unless he is led captive by the delight of prosperity.

The seventh and last petition is "But deliver us from evil" (Mt. 6:13). We are to pray not only that we may not be led into the evil from which we are free, which is asked in the sixth petition, but that we may also be delivered from that into which we have been already led. And when this has been done, nothing frightening will remain, nor will any temptation at all have to be feared. And yet in this life, so long as we carry about our present mortality, into which we were led by the persuasion of the serpent, it is not to be hoped that this can be the case, yet we are to hope that at some future time it will take place. And this is the hope which is not seen, of which the apostle said, "Now hope that is seen is not hope" (Rom. 8:24). Yet the wisdom which is granted in this life also is not to be despaired of by the faithful servants of God. With the most wary vigilance, we should shun what we have understood (from the Lord's revealing it) is to be shunned; and with the most ardent love, we should seek what we have understood (from the Lord's revealing it) is to be sought after. Thus, after the remaining burden of this mortality has been laid down in the act of dying, there shall be perfected in every part of man at the fit time the blessedness which has begun in this life, and which we have from time to time strained every nerve to lay hold of and secure.

The distinction among these seven petitions ought to be considered and commended. Our temporal life is being spent now, and what is eternal is being hoped for; eternal things are superior in dignity, even if it is only when we are finished with temporal things that we pass to eternal things. The first three petitions begin to be answered in this life, which is spent in the present world. The hallowing of God's name begins with the coming of the Lord of humility; the coming of His Kingdom, to which He will come in splendor, will be manifested not after the end of the world, but in the end of the world; and the perfect doing of His will on earth as in heaven (whether you understand by "heaven and earth" the "righteous and sinners," or "spirit and flesh," or the "Lord and the Church," or all these things together) will be brought to completion with the perfecting of our blessedness, and therefore at the close of the world. Yet all three will remain even in eternity. The hallowing of God's name will go on for ever; there is no end of His Kingdom; and eternal life is promised to our perfected blessedness. Hence, those three things will remain consummated and thoroughly completed in that life which is promised us.

But the other four things which we ask seem to me to belong to this temporal life. The first of them is "Give us this day our daily bread" (Mt. 6:11). Whether by this thing which is called daily bread is meant spiritual bread, or what is visible in the Sacrament, or our sustenance, "daily bread" belongs to the present time, which He has called "today," not because spiritual food is not everlasting, but because what is called daily food in the Scriptures is made present to the soul either by the sound of the expression or by temporal signs. Such temporal signs will certainly no longer exist when all will be "taught by God" (Jn. 6:45; cf. Is. 54:13), and thus all will no longer teach others by movement of their bodies, but each one for himself by the purity of his mind will drink in the ineffable light of Truth Itself. Perhaps there is another reason why it is called bread, not drink: because bread is converted into nourishment by breaking and masticating it (just as the Scriptures feed the soul by being opened up and made the subject of discourse), but drink, when prepared, passes as it is into the body. At present, then, the truth is bread, when it is called "daily bread"; but it will be drink when there will be no need of the labor of discussing and discoursing (as it were of breaking and masticating), but merely of drinking unmingled and transparent truth.

And sins are at present forgiven us, and at present we forgive them—this is the second petition of the four that remain—but then there will be no pardon of sins, because there will be no sins. And temptations assault us in this temporal life, but they will have no existence when the words "Thou shalt hide them in the secret of thy face" (Ps. 30:21, Douay Rheims Version) will be fully realized. And the evil from which we wish to be delivered, as well as the deliverance from evil itself, belongs certainly to this life. Being mortal, we have deserved evil at the hand of God's justice, and we are delivered from it by His mercy.

The sevenfold number of these petitions also seems to me to correspond to that sevenfold number out of which the whole sermon before us [the Sermon on the Mount] has arisen. If the poor in spirit are blessed through the fear of God, inasmuch as theirs is the Kingdom of Heaven, then let us ask that the name of God be hallowed among men because "the fear of the LORD is clean, enduring for ever" (Ps. 19:9).

If the meek are blessed through piety, inasmuch as they shall inherit the earth, then let us ask that His Kingdom come, whether it be over ourselves (that we may become meek, and not resist Him), or whether it be from heaven to earth in the splendor of the Lord's Advent, in which we shall rejoice and be praised when He says, "Come, O blessed of my Father, inherit the kingdom prepared for you from the foundation of the world" (Mt. 25:34). For the prophet says, "My soul makes its boast in the LORD; let the afflicted hear and be glad" (Ps. 34:2).

If those who mourn are blessed through knowledge, inasmuch as they shall be comforted, then let us pray that His will be done on earth as it is in heaven, because when the body (which is, as it were, the earth) shall agree in a final and complete peace with the soul (which is, as it were, heaven), we shall not mourn, for there is no other mourning belonging to this present time, except when these contend against each other and compel us to say, "I see in my members another law at war with the law of my mind," and compel us to testify our grief with tearful voice, "Wretched man that I am! Who will deliver me from this body of death?" (Rom. 7:23, 24).

If those who hunger and thirst after righteousness are blessed through fortitude, inasmuch as they shall be filled, then let us pray that our daily bread may be given to us today; may we, supported and sustained by this bread, be able to reach that most abundant fullness.

If the merciful are blessed through prudence, inasmuch as they shall obtain mercy, then let us forgive our debtors their debts, and let us pray that ours may be forgiven us.

If the pure in heart are blessed through understanding, inasmuch as they shall see God, then let us pray not to be led into temptation, lest we should have a double heart in not seeking after a single good to which we may refer all our actions, but instead in pursuing things temporal and earthly. For temptations arising from those things that seem to men burdensome and calamitous have no power over us, if those other temptations that befall us through the enticements of things that men count as good and cause for rejoicing have no power.

If the peacemakers are blessed through wisdom, inasmuch as they shall be called the children of God, then let us pray that we may be freed from evil, for that very freedom will make us free, that is, sons of God, so that we may cry in the spirit of adoption, "Abba! Father!" (Rom. 8:15; Gal. 4:6).

Nor indeed are we to pass carelessly by the circumstance that of all those petitions in which the Lord has taught us to pray, He has judged that the one which has reference to the forgiveness of sins is chiefly to be commended. In it, He would have us be merciful, because mercy is the only wisdom for escaping misery. In no other petition do we pray that we, as it were, enter into a covenant with God, for we say, "[F]orgive us our debts, [a]s we also have forgiven our debtors" (Mt. 6:12). And if we lie in that covenant, the whole prayer is fruitless. He says, "For if you forgive men their trespasses, your heavenly Father also will forgive you; but if you do not forgive men their trespasses, neither will your Father forgive your trespasses" (Mt. 6:14).

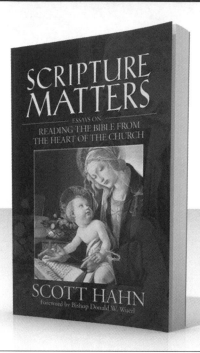

CONCRETE EXPERIENCES
OF MARRIED COUPLES WHO STRIVE TO LIVE OUT THEIR VOCATION DAY BY DAY

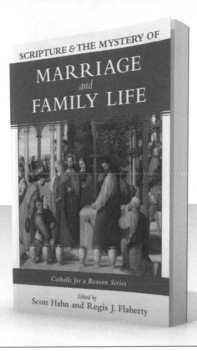

SCRIPTURE AND THE MYSTERY OF MARRIAGE AND FAMILY LIFE
EDITED BY SCOTT HAHN & REGIS J. FLAHERTY

Marriage and family life lived according to God's plan can change lives and change the world. In this exploration of the scriptural basis of God's plan for the family, Scott and Kimberly Hahn, Mike and Terri Aquilina, and other Catholic authors and their spouses testify to the joys, struggles, and sanctity found in marriage. Essays include *The World as Wedding*, *Lessons Learned at Nazareth*, and *Reflections on Pope Benedict XVI's First Encyclical*. Find encouragement from these lessons on the covenant of marriage, parenting, sexuality, and much more.

EMMAUS ROAD PUBLISHING

Call **740-264-9535** to order or visit **EmmausRoad.org**

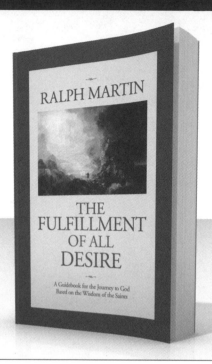